MW00946657

Low Cholesterol Cookbook for Beginners

1800 Days of Simple & Delicious Recipes to Support
Cardiovascular Management and Enhance Heart Health,
Featuring a Comprehensive 60-Day Meal Plan

Pamela Adkins

Copyright Statement and Disclaimer © 2024 by Pamela Adkins. All rights reserved.

No part of this book titled "Low Cholesterol Cookbook for Beginners: 1800 Days of Simple & Delicious Recipes to Support Cardiovascular Management and Enhance Heart Health, Featuring a Comprehensive 60-Day Meal Plan" may be copied, distributed, or transmitted in any way without the publisher's prior written consent. The only exceptions are condensed quotations used in critical evaluations and specific non-commercial uses allowed by copyright law. This includes photocopying, recording, and other electronic or mechanical methods.

The information provided in this book is for educational and informational purposes only and is not intended as medical advice. The information provided here should be used outside expert medical advice, diagnosis, or care. For any queries about a medical problem, you should always consult your doctor or another trained health expert.

Any liability resulting from using this book, whether direct or indirect, is disclaimed by the publisher and author. The recipes and nutritional information provided are based on the author's research and personal experience and are not guaranteed to be suitable for all individuals.

Publisher: Pamela Adkins

First Edition: 2024

Printed in the United States of America

Table of Contents

Introduction

Welcome to "Low Cholesterol Cookbook for Beginners," your gateway to a healthier lifestyle through heart-friendly eating. This book is your starting point for lowering cholesterol, preventing heart disease, or adopting a more nutritious diet. We understand that altering your diet can be intimidating., but we're here to show you how manageable and enjoyable they can be.

Cholesterol is a waxy substance in your blood, vital for creating cells and hormones. However, too much bad cholesterol (LDL) can lead to heart disease and strokes by building up in the arteries. Fortunately, diet is one of the most effective cholesterol management methods. This cookbook aims to equip you with the knowledge and recipes to do just that.

A low-cholesterol diet isn't just about avoiding certain foods—it's about focusing on foods that can help improve your heart health. This includes many fruits, vegetables, whole grains, and lean proteins. By embracing these foods, you can reduce your LDL cholesterol levels and significantly lower your risk of heart disease.

This cookbook is designed to make heart-healthy eating accessible and enjoyable. You'll find simple, practical recipes that don't require hard-to-find ingredients or complex cooking methods. Transitioning to a low-cholesterol diet doesn't have to be a sacrifice of flavor or enjoyment. Each of our dishes caters to your health needs and delights your taste buds.

As you embark on this gastronomic adventure, remember that each recipe is more than just a meal—it's a step towards a healthier heart and a more vibrant life. We've tailored this cookbook to help you confidently navigate your dietary choices, whether cooking for one or preparing a meal for the whole family.

We invite you to dive into these pages with enthusiasm and curiosity. The changes you make today have the power to transform your health tomorrow. Let this cookbook guide you in lowering cholesterol and embracing a diet that nourishes and satisfies you. A heart-healthy life awaits, one delicious meal at a time!

Chapter 1. Introduction to Low Cholesterol Eating

1.1 The Nature of Cholesterol

Cholesterol is a waxy, fat-like substance found in all body cells. It's essential for producing cell membranes, certain hormones, and vitamin D. Despite its bad reputation, cholesterol is vital to your body's daily functioning because it is one of the most potent antioxidants. Approximately 15% of cholesterol enters your body with food; the liver produces the remaining 85%.

Cholesterol travels through your bloodstream in small packages called lipoproteins, which are made of fat (lipids) and proteins on the outside.

There are several types of cholesterol, classified based on the kind of lipoprotein that carries them:

1.   Low-Density Lipoprotein (LDL): Often called 'bad' cholesterol, LDL carries cholesterol from the liver to the cells that require it.

2.   High-Density Lipoprotein (HDL): Often referred to as 'good' cholesterol, HDL transports cholesterol from the cells to the liver, which is either metabolized or expelled as a waste substance

1.2 The Difference Between Good vs. Bad Cholesterol

Let's analyze in detail the difference between the two types of lipoproteins that transport cholesterol throughout your body in this section:

Low-density lipoprotein (LDL): Often called "bad" cholesterol, LDL carries cholesterol from the liver to the cells. Excess LDL cholesterol in the bloodstream can gradually accumulate in the artery walls that supply the heart and brain.

Critical Points of LDL:
- LDL carries cholesterol to arteries.
- High LDL levels can lead to plaque buildup and heart disease.

High-Density Lipoprotein (HDL): Known as "good" cholesterol, HDL transports cholesterol from the cells back to the liver, where it is either degraded or expelled from the body as waste. High levels of HDL cholesterol can decrease the risk of heart disease.

Critical Points of HDL:
- HDL carries cholesterol away from arteries to the liver.
- High HDL levels are beneficial and reduce the risk of cardiovascular diseases.
- Impact on Health

Preserving a healthy equilibrium between LDL and HDL can significantly decrease the likelihood of plaque accumulation and enhance the health of the arteries. An imbalance, exceptionally high LDL, and low HDL can lead to severe health issues, including coronary artery disease.

1.3 The Role of Diet in Heart Health

High cholesterol does not cause symptoms; hence, it's often termed a "silent" condition. However, over time, if levels remain elevated, it increases the risk of cardiovascular diseases, including:

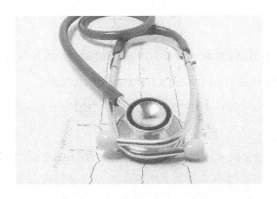

- Heart attack,

- Stroke,

- Peripheral artery disease.

These conditions stem from atherosclerosis, a process in which cholesterol and other substances build up on artery walls, forming plaques that narrow and block blood flow.

Eating well is one of the most effective tools for combating heart disease, the leading cause of death worldwide. Your diet plays a significant role in managing cholesterol levels and maintaining overall heart health. This chapter explores how the foods you eat—and those you choose to avoid—can influence your heart's well-being.

❖ Nutrients and Heart Health

A heart-healthy diet involves a variety of nutrients that work together to protect your cardiovascular system. This section will discuss the roles of critical nutrients such as:

Healthy Fats: Not all fats are bad. Omega-3 fatty acids and monounsaturated fats can help reduce blood pressure and lower triglyceride levels.

Fiber: Soluble fiber helps reduce the absorption of cholesterol into your bloodstream.

Antioxidants: These compounds help combat oxidative stress, which can lead to arterial damage.

❖ Foods That Promote Heart Health

Certain foods are particularly beneficial for heart health. This section provides a list of must-have foods in a heart-healthy diet, including:

Leafy Greens: Rich in vitamins, minerals, and antioxidants.

Whole Grains: Full of fiber that helps lower cholesterol and maintain blood sugar levels.

Berries and Nuts: Great sources of antioxidants and healthy fats.

❖ Modifying Your Diet for Better Heart Health!

A. Reducing Bad Fats and Cholesterol

This section explains the importance of reducing the intake of saturated and trans fats, which contribute to high levels of bad cholesterol and are major risk factors for heart disease.

Identifying Sources of Bad Fats: Learn how to read labels to avoid hidden sources in processed foods.

Healthy Substitutions: Avoid unhealthy fats for more nutritious options without sacrificing flavor.

B. Incorporating Plant-Based Meals

Boosting the ratio of plant-based foods in your diet can enhance cardiac health. This section offers:

Benefits of a Plant-Based Diet Include reduced blood pressure and lower cholesterol.

Tips for Starting: Gradually introduce more plant-based meals into your routine.

C. Portion Control and Meal Planning

Understanding portion sizes and planning meals can help you manage weight, reduce cholesterol, and decrease heart disease risk.

Portion Sizes: Guidelines on how to measure portions accurately.

Meal Planning: Strategies for preparing heart-healthy meals throughout the week.

Diet is a powerful tool in the fight against heart disease. By understanding how different foods and nutrients affect your heart, you can make choices that enhance your health and well-being. Embrace these changes as a diet and a sustainable lifestyle for lasting heart health.

1.4 Foods that Lower Cholesterol

This chapter delves into the variety of foods proven to lower cholesterol, offering insights on how to integrate them effectively into daily meals.

Fruits and Vegetables

- Rich in Fiber and Antioxidants: Fruits and vegetables are essential to a low-cholesterol diet. They are high in dietary fiber, which helps reduce cholesterol absorption in the bloodstream.
- Best Choices: Incorporate a variety of colorful vegetables like leafy greens, bell peppers, and carrots, along with fruits such as apples, berries, and pears that are high in pectin, a type of soluble fiber that assists in cholesterol reduction.

Whole Grains

- Full of Soluble Fiber: Whole grains like oats, barley, and whole wheat contain beta-glucan, a soluble fiber that effectively lowers cholesterol.
- Incorporating Whole Grains: Start your day with oatmeal, use whole-grain bread for sandwiches, and choose whole-wheat pasta or brown rice as side dishes.

Nuts and Seeds

- A Heart-Healthy Snack: Nuts and seeds are good sources of unsaturated fats, which can help reduce bad cholesterol (LDL) and raise good cholesterol (HDL).
- Types to Include: Almonds, walnuts, flaxseeds, and chia seeds are not only tasty but also beneficial for heart health. Just be mindful of the portion sizes, as nuts are high in calories.

Legumes

• Versatile and Nutritious: Legumes, including beans, peas, and lentils, are excellent sources of soluble fiber and protein. They can be used in various dishes, from salads to soups, and they provide cholesterol-lowering benefits and heart health support.

Fatty Fish

• Omega-3 Fatty Acids: Fatty fish like salmon, mackerel, and sardines are rich in omega-3 fatty acids and are known for improving heart health by reducing triglycerides and lowering blood pressure.

• Cooking and Serving Tips: Grilling, baking, or steaming fish are healthy ways to enjoy its benefits without adding unhealthy fats.

Plant-based Oils

• Healthy Fats: Substituting saturated fats with unsaturated fats in plant-derived oils such as olive oil, canola oil, and avocado oil can help reduce cholesterol levels.

• Usage Tips: Use these oils in cooking and salad dressings instead of butter, cream, or lard.

Soy

• A Protein Alternative: Soy products such as tofu, soy milk, and edamame can help reduce cholesterol. They contain isoflavones, which are believed to lower LDL cholesterol.

• Incorporating Soy into Your Diet: Substitute meat with tofu in stir-fry dishes, enjoy soy milk in smoothies, and add edamame to salads for a nutritious boost.

Understanding which foods can help lower cholesterol and how to incorporate them into your diet can significantly improve your cardiovascular health. This chapter provides the foundation for making informed choices about the foods you eat every day, helping you manage your cholesterol levels effectively and deliciously.

1.5 Foods that increase Cholesterol

In the journey to maintain a healthy heart and lower cholesterol levels, it's crucial to identify and minimize foods that can negatively impact your lipid profile. This chapter will explore foods detrimental to cholesterol levels and offer guidance on avoiding or replacing them in your diet.

1. Trans Fats

• Industrial Culprits: Often found in processed snacks, baked goods, and certain margarines, trans fats are notorious for increasing the risk of heart disease by raising harmful cholesterol levels and lowering good cholesterol.

• Avoidance Strategies: Learn to read labels for terms like "partially hydrogenated oils" and aim to eliminate these from your diet.

2. Saturated Fats

• Familiar Sources: Red meats, full-fat dairy products, butter, and cheese contain high saturated fats.

• Moderation Tips: While it's not necessary to eliminate these foods, it's crucial to limit their intake. Opt for lean cuts of meat and low-fat dairy options, and use plant-based oils for cooking.

3. Processed Meats

• Unhealthy Choices: Sausages, bacon, and processed deli meats are high in cholesterol and saturated fats.

• Healthier Alternatives: Choose lean protein sources like chicken, turkey, or fish. When selecting red meat, look for 90% lean or higher cuts.

4. Fast Food

• Dietary Downfalls: Fast food is often laden with trans fats, saturated fats, and excessive calories.

• Eating Out, Eating Right: Opt for healthier choices like salads with grilled proteins and vinaigrette on the side or a grilled chicken sandwich without mayonnaise.

5. Desserts and Sweets

• Sugar and Fats Collide: Cakes, cookies, ice cream, and pastries not only contribute to higher cholesterol but also lead to weight gain, which is another risk factor for heart disease.

• Sweet Substitutions: Satisfy your sweet tooth with fruits, dark chocolate, or non-dairy frozen desserts made from almond or coconut milk.

6. Full-Fat Dairy Products

• Caloric Concerns: Items like whole milk, cream, and high-fat cheeses are high in saturated fats.

• Smarter Dairy Decisions: Switch to skim or 1% milk, enjoy low-fat yogurts, and use cheese sparingly.

7. Fried Foods

• Crispy Consequences: Fried foods are typically cooked in oils loaded with trans fats or saturated fats.

• Better Cooking Methods: Baking, grilling, or air frying can provide tasty alternatives that don't compromise your cholesterol levels.

Navigating the pitfalls of high-cholesterol foods requires diligence and a willingness to make healthier dietary choices. Understanding what foods to avoid and how to substitute them with healthier alternatives can significantly improve your lipid levels and overall heart health. This chapter aims to give you the knowledge to make those choices effectively, ensuring your diet supports your heart health goals.

1.6 Cholesterol-Lowering Supplements

Supplements can support diet and exercise in maintaining a heart-healthy lifestyle. This chapter explores various cholesterol-lowering supplements, their benefits, and how to integrate them safely into your daily regimen.

Before incorporating any supplements into your routine, it's crucial to understand what they are and how they work. Supplements for lowering cholesterol typically aim to reduce cholesterol absorption in the gut, decrease the production of cholesterol in the liver, or increase the removal of cholesterol from the blood.

Popular Supplements and Their Mechanisms:

• *Plant Sterols and Stanols:* These substances, similar in structure to cholesterol, help block cholesterol absorption in the intestine. Regular intake can lead to a modest reduction in LDL cholesterol.

- *Omega-3 Fatty Acids:* In fish oil and flaxseeds, omega-3s help reduce triglyceride levels in the bloodstream and improve heart health by enhancing cardiovascular function.

- *Psyllium* is a fiber that helps lower LDL cholesterol by binding with bile acids in the digestive system. It encourages the liver to use excess cholesterol to produce more bile acids, thus reducing the level of cholesterol in the blood.

- *Red Yeast Rice* includes monacolin K, chemically the same as the active component in certain cholesterol-reducing statin drugs. Nonetheless, the amount of monacolin K can differ significantly among various supplements.

1. Efficacy and Research

Discuss the scientific evidence supporting each supplement's efficacy in cholesterol management. Highlight studies that provide insight into how these supplements compare to traditional medications.

2. Potential Risks and Side Effects

While supplements can be beneficial, they are not free from risks. Detail possible side effects and interactions with other medications. Highlight the necessity of discussing with a healthcare professional before beginning any new supplement, particularly for individuals already on prescribed medications.

3. Integrating Supplements into a Low-Cholesterol Diet

Guide how to combine dietary changes and supplements effectively. Discuss timing, dosage, and the importance of consistency in taking supplements.

4. Conclusion

Summarize the role of supplements in managing cholesterol levels and reiterate the importance of a comprehensive approach that includes diet, exercise, and regular medical check-ups.

This chapter will help readers make informed decisions about using supplements as part of their strategy to lower cholesterol and enhance overall heart health.

1.7 Tips for Eating Out and Staying Low Cholesterol

Eating out can be one of the biggest challenges when managing cholesterol levels. This chapter provides practical tips to help you make heart-healthy choices at restaurants, ensuring you can enjoy dining out without compromising your dietary goals.

1. Preparing to Dine Out

• Research Ahead: Before visiting a restaurant, check its menu online. Many places provide nutritional information, allowing you to choose dishes that align with your low-cholesterol diet.

• Ask Questions: Don't hesitate to ask the restaurant staff about the ingredients or cooking methods of their dishes. Understanding what goes into your meal can help you make healthier choices.

2. Making Smart Menu Choices

• Opt for Grilled or Baked: Grilled, baked, or steamed dishes are typically lower in unhealthy fats than fried or creamy.

• Watch Your Portions: Restaurant portions can be larger than standard serving sizes. Consider sharing a dish with a dining companion or asking for a half portion.

• Salads and Vegetables: Start with a salad dressed with olive oil and vinegar or lemon juice, and fill half your plate with vegetables to keep calorie and cholesterol intake in check.

3. Understanding Menu Terms

• Foods to Choose: Look for keywords like "steamed," "broiled," "grilled," "baked," and "roasted." These cooking methods usually involve less oil and fat.

• Foods to Avoid: Avoid terms like "fried," "crispy," "creamy," "buttered," and "breaded," as these often indicate higher fat and cholesterol content.

4. Customizing Your Order

• Modify Your Meal: Request modifications to your dish, such as dressing on the side, no added salt, or swapping outsides (e.g., choosing steamed vegetables instead of French fries).

• Skip the Extras: Avoid high-cholesterol extras such as bacon bits, cheese, or creamy sauces.

5. Handling Fast Food

• Better Choices in Fast Food: Opt for salads, wraps, or grilled chicken sandwiches. Avoid large sizes and combo meals that can lead to overeating.

6. Be Beverage-Wise

• Drinks to Consider: Choose water, unsweetened tea, or other non-caloric beverages. Avoid sugary drinks and excessive alcohol, which can contribute to higher triglyceride levels.

7. Desserts

• Sweet Endings: If you desire something sweet, look for fruit-based desserts or share a dessert to satisfy your craving without overindulging.

Eating out doesn't have to derail your low-cholesterol diet. With careful choices and minor modifications, you can enjoy a social and satisfying meal while keeping your health on track. Remember that sporadic treats are elements of a balanced lifestyle, yet being conscious of your selections will aid in upholding your dietary objectives.

This chapter empowers readers with the knowledge and strategies they need to confidently navigate menus and make healthy choices, ensuring that dining out remains a pleasurable and heart-healthy experience.

Chapter 2.Breakfasts

Avocado Toast with Tomatoes

Prep. time: 5 min | Cook time: 2 min | Serves: 2

Ingredients

- 2 slices of whole-grain bread
- 1 ripe avocado
- 1 small tomato, sliced
- Juice of half a lemon
- Salt and black pepper to taste
- Optional garnishes: fresh basil leaves, a sprinkle of crushed red pepper flakes

Directions

1. Toast the Bread: Toast the bread slices until golden and crisp.
2. Prepare the Avocado: In a small bowl, mash the avocado with salt, black pepper, and lemon juice until creamy and smooth.
3. Assemble: Spread the mashed avocado evenly over the toasted bread slices. Top each with sliced tomatoes, arranging them neatly.
4. Garnish and Serve: Add fresh basil and a sprinkle of red pepper flakes if desired. Serve immediately for the best taste.

Nutritional Information:
Calories: 260, Protein: 7 g, Carbohydrates: 30 g, Fat: 14 g, Fiber: 9 g, Cholesterol: 0 mg, Sodium: 210 mg, Potassium: 510 mg

Oatmeal with berries and almonds

Prep. time: 5 min | Cook time: 10 min | Serves: 4

Ingredients

- 2 cups rolled oats
- 4 cups water or unsweetened almond milk
- 1 cup mixed berries (fresh or frozen)
- 1/4 cup sliced almonds
- 1 tablespoon honey or maple syrup
- 1/2 teaspoon cinnamon (optional)

Directions

1. Cook Oatmeal: Bring the water or almond milk to a boil in a medium saucepan. Add the rolled oats and lower the heat to a simmer. Cook for approximately 10 minutes, stirring now and then, until the oats are tender and have soaked up much of the liquid.
2. Add Flavors: Stir in the cinnamon and honey (or maple syrup) until well combined.
3. Prepare Berries: If using frozen berries, add them directly to the hot oatmeal to thaw. If using fresh berries, rinse them under cold water.
4. Serve: Spoon the oatmeal into bowls. Top each serving with a quarter of the mixed berries and a tablespoon of sliced almonds.
5. Enjoy: Serve hot, with additional honey or syrup if desired for extra sweetness.

Nutritional Information:
Calories: 290, Protein: 9 g, Carbohydrates: 45 g, Fat: 9 g, Fiber: 7 g, Cholesterol: 0 mg, Sodium: 30 mg, Potassium: 350 mg

Banana Pancakes

Prep. time: 10 min | Cook time: 15 min | Serves: 4

Ingredients

- 2 ripe bananas, mashed
- 1 cup whole wheat flour
- 1 tablespoon baking powder
- 1/4 teaspoon salt
- 1 cup unsweetened almond milk
- 2 tablespoons olive oil
- 1 egg (or 2 egg whites for lower cholesterol)
- 1 teaspoon vanilla extract
- Optional: 1/2 teaspoon cinnamon

Directions

1. Mix Dry Ingredients: In a large bowl, combine the whole wheat flour, salt, baking powder, and cinnamon (if using).
2. Combine Wet Ingredients: In another bowl, whisk together the mashed bananas, almond milk, olive oil, egg (or egg whites), and vanilla extract.
3. Make the Batter: Pour the wet ingredients into the dry ingredients and stir until combined. The batter should be slightly lumpy.
4. Cook the Pancakes: Warm a non-stick frying pan over medium heat. Add 1/4 cup of batter for each pancake and cook until bubbles appear on the surface, roughly 2-3 minutes. Turn over and continue to cook for another 2 minutes or until they are golden brown.
5. Serve: Serve hot with your choice of toppings, such as fresh fruit, a drizzle of honey, or a sprinkle of nuts.

Nutritional Information:
Calories: 230, Protein: 6 g, Carbohydrates: 36 g, Fat: 8 g, Fiber: 4 g, Cholesterol: 53 mg, Sodium: 300 mg, Potassium: 422 mg

Quinoa and Berry Breakfast Bowl

Prep. time: 5 min | Cook time: 15 min | Serves: 4

Ingredients

- 1 cup quinoa, rinsed
- 2 cups water
- 1 cup mixed berries (such as strawberries, blueberries, and raspberries)
- 1/4 cup sliced almonds
- 1/4 cup chia seeds
- 2 tablespoons honey or maple syrup
- Optional: 1/2 teaspoon cinnamon or vanilla extract for flavor

Directions

1. Cook Quinoa: Combine the rinsed quinoa and water in a medium saucepan. Bring to a boil, then cover and reduce heat to a simmer. Cook for about 15 minutes or until the quinoa is tender and the water has been absorbed.
2. Flavor the Quinoa: Remove from heat. If desired, stir in cinnamon or vanilla extract for added flavor.
3. Prepare the Bowl: Divide the cooked quinoa among four bowls. Top each bowl evenly with mixed berries, sliced almonds, and chia seeds.
4. Sweeten and Serve: Drizzle honey or maple syrup over each bowl. Serve warm or at room temperature.

Nutritional Information:
Calories: 290, Protein: 9 g, Carbohydrates: 49 g, Fat: 7 g, Fiber: 8 g, Cholesterol: 0 mg, Sodium: 13 mg, Potassium: 410 mg

Banana Nut Smoothie

Prep. time: 5 min | Cook time: 0 min | Serves: 2

Ingredients

- 2 ripe bananas
- 2 tablespoons almond butter
- 1 cup unsweetened almond milk
- 1/2 teaspoon vanilla extract
- 1/4 cup rolled oats
- 2 teaspoons honey (optional)
- 1 tablespoon ground flaxseed
- Ice cubes (optional)

Directions

1. Combine Ingredients: In a blender, place bananas, almond butter, almond milk, vanilla extract, rolled oats, honey if using, and flaxseed. Add ice if desired for a thicker smoothie.
2. Blend: Blend on high until smooth, stopping to scrape down the sides if necessary.
3. Taste and Adjust: Taste the smoothie; add more honey for sweetness if desired.
4. Serve: Divide the smoothie between two glasses and serve immediately.

Nutritional Information:
Calories: 295, Protein: 6 g, Carbohydrates: 43 g, Fat: 11 g, Fiber: 5 g, Cholesterol: 0 mg, Sodium: 80 mg, Potassium: 600 mg

Chia Pudding Parfait

Prep. time: 15 min | Cook time: 0 min (plus 4 hours refrigeration) | Serves: 4

Ingredients

- 1/4 cup chia seeds
- 1 cup unsweetened almond milk
- 1 tablespoon honey or maple syrup
- 1/2 teaspoon vanilla extract
- 1 cup mixed berries (blueberries, raspberries, and strawberries)
- 1/2 cup granola (low-fat, low-sugar)

Directions

1. Prepare the Chia Pudding: In a bowl, combine the chia seeds, almond milk, honey (or maple syrup), and vanilla extract. Stir thoroughly to mix. Let the mixture sit for about 5 minutes, then stir again to prevent clumping. Cover and refrigerate for at least 4 hours or overnight until it achieves a pudding-like consistency.
2. Layer the Parfait: Take four serving glasses. Spoon a layer of chia pudding into each glass, followed by a layer of mixed berries. Add a layer of granola on top of the berries.
3. Repeat the Layers: Repeat the layering process until all ingredients are used up, finishing with a top layer of berries.
4. Serve: Serve immediately or cover and keep refrigerated until ready to serve.

Nutritional Information:
Calories: 180, Protein: 4 g, Carbohydrates: 24 g, Fat: 8 g, Fiber: 6 g, Cholesterol: 0 mg, Sodium: 30 mg, Potassium: 150 mg

Smoothie with chia seeds and kiwi

Prep. time: 10 min | Cook time: 0 min | Serves: 2

Ingredients

- 2 ripe kiwis, peeled and quartered
- 1 banana, sliced
- 1 cup fresh spinach leaves
- 1 tablespoon chia seeds
- 1/2 cup unsweetened almond milk
- 1/2 cup Greek yogurt, plain
- 1 tablespoon honey (optional for sweetness)
- Ice cubes (optional for a thicker smoothie)

Directions

1. Prepare Ingredients: Blend kiwis, banana, spinach, chia seeds, almond milk, Greek yogurt, and honey.
2. Blend: Add ice cubes if using, and blend on high until smooth and creamy. If necessary, modify the consistency by incorporating additional almond milk.
3. Taste and Fine-tune: Sample the smoothie and mix in more honey if a sweeter flavor is preferred.
4. Serve at Once: Transfer the smoothie into glasses and serve instantly to ensure optimal taste and nutrient preservation.

Nutritional Information:
Calories: 190, Protein: 8 g, Carbohydrates: 35 g, Fat: 3 g, Fiber: 6 g, Cholesterol: 5 mg, Sodium: 55 mg, Potassium: 500 mg

Mediterranean Veggie Omelette

Prep. time: 10 min | Cook time: 8 min | Serves: 4

Ingredients

- 4 large egg whites
- 1 whole egg
- 1/2 cup chopped spinach
- 1/4 cup diced tomatoes
- 1/4 cup sliced black olives
- 1/4 cup crumbled feta cheese
- 1 tablespoon chopped fresh basil
- 1 tablespoon olive oil
- Salt and pepper to taste

Directions

1. Prepare the Eggs: Whisk together the egg whites and whole egg until thoroughly combined, seasoning with salt and pepper.
2. Cook the Vegetables: Heat the olive oil in a non-stick skillet over medium heat. Add the spinach, tomatoes, olives, and sauté for about 2 minutes until the spinach is wilted.
3. Add the Egg Mixture: Pour the egg mixture over the sautéed vegetables in the skillet. Cook for about 3 minutes or until the eggs are on the bottom.
4. Add Cheese and Basil: Sprinkle the feta cheese and chopped basil over half of the omelet. Fold the other half over the cheese and basil.
5. Finish Cooking: The omelet should be cooked for 2-3 minutes until the cheese melts. Carefully slide the omelet onto a plate to serve.

Nutritional Information:
Calories: 230, Protein: 20 g, Carbohydrates: 6 g, Fat: 14 g, Fiber: 2 g, Cholesterol: 110 mg, Sodium: 590 mg, Potassium: 300 mg

Greek yogurt with honey and nuts

Prep. time: 5 min | Cook time: 0 min | Serves: 4

Ingredients

- 2 cups Greek yogurt, low-fat
- 4 tablespoons honey
- 1/2 cup mixed nuts (almonds, walnuts, and pecans), roughly chopped
- Optional: a pinch of cinnamon or vanilla extract for flavoring

Directions

1. Prepare the Ingredients: If using whole nuts, chop them roughly to get about 1/2 cup. Set it aside.
2. Mix Yogurt and Honey: Combine Greek yogurt with honey in a bowl. Add a pinch of cinnamon or a few drops of vanilla extract if desired, and mix well until thoroughly combined.
3. Add Nuts: Stir the chopped nuts into the yogurt mixture or sprinkle them on top before serving for added crunch.
4. Serve: Divide the yogurt into serving bowls. Drizzle with a little more honey and top with additional nuts if preferred. Serve immediately or chill before serving for a refreshing snack.

Nutritional Information:
Calories: 220, Protein: 12 g, Carbohydrates: 18 g, Fat: 10 g, Fiber: 2 g, Cholesterol: 10 mg, Sodium: 45 mg, Potassium: 160 mg

Almond Butter and Banana Toast

Prep. time: 5 min | Cook time: 2 min | Serves: 4

Ingredients

- 4 slices of whole-grain bread
- 1/4 cup almond butter
- 2 ripe bananas, sliced
- Optional toppings: chia seeds, honey, cinnamon

Directions

1. Toast the whole grain bread slices until golden and crispy.
2. Evenly spread almond butter on each slice of toasted bread.
3. Arrange banana slices on top of the almond butter.
4. If desired, sprinkle with chia seeds, drizzle with honey, and dust with cinnamon.
5. Serve: For the most flavor and texture, serve right away.

Nutritional Information:
Calories: 280, Protein: 8g, Carbohydrates: 38g, Fat: 12g, Fiber: 6g, Cholesterol: 0mg, Sodium: 200mg, Potassium: 450mg

Poached Eggs with Avocado Salad

Prep. time: 15 min | Cook time: 10 min | Serves: 4

Ingredients

- 4 large eggs
- 2 avocados, diced
- 1 cup cherry tomatoes, halved
- 1/4 red onion, thinly sliced
- 2 cups mixed salad greens
- 1 tablespoon olive oil
- 1 tablespoon white vinegar (for poaching)
- Juice of 1 lime
- Salt and pepper, to taste
- Chopped fresh herbs (parsley, cilantro, etc.)

Directions

1. Fill a medium saucepan with water, add white vinegar, and bring to a gentle simmer.
2. Split every egg into a tiny bowl and gently slide it into the simmering water. Poach the eggs for about 3-4 minutes for soft yolks or longer for firmer yolks.
3. While the eggs poach, combine the diced avocados, cherry tomatoes, red onion, and salad greens in a large bowl.
4. Drizzle olive oil and lime juice over the salad. Add salt and pepper to taste, then softly toss to combine.
5. Using a slotted spoon, remove the eggs and place them on paper towels to drain.
6. Divide the salad among plates and top each with a poached egg. Sprinkle with fresh herbs before serving.

Nutritional information:
Calories: 290, Protein: 10g, Carbohydrates: 12g, Fat: 23g, Fiber: 7g, Cholesterol: 185mg, Sodium: 210mg, Potassium: 650mg.

Egg White Veggie Scramble

Prep. time: 10 min | Cook time: 10 min | Serves: 4

Ingredients

- 8 large egg whites
- 1 tablespoon olive oil
- 1 red bell pepper, diced
- 1 small onion, diced
- 1 cup mushrooms, sliced
- 1 cup fresh spinach, roughly chopped
- Salt and pepper to taste
- Optional: 1/4 teaspoon garlic powder or fresh minced garlic for extra flavor

Directions

1. Prepare the Vegetables: Heat olive oil in a non-stick skillet over medium heat. Add the diced onion and bell pepper. Cook for about 3 minutes until they start to soften. Add the mushrooms and cook for another 2 minutes.
2. Cook Egg Whites: In a bowl, lightly beat the egg whites with salt, pepper, and garlic powder. Pour the egg whites over the sautéed vegetables in the skillet and let them sit for about 1 minute without stirring.
3. Scramble: As the edges begin to set, gently stir the mixture, folding the egg whites over the vegetables. Continue cooking for another 3-4 minutes until the egg whites are fully cooked and no liquid remains.
4. Add Spinach: Stir in the chopped spinach and cook for an additional minute until the spinach is wilted.
5. Serve: Adjust seasoning if necessary, and serve hot.

Nutritional Information:
Calories: 120, Protein: 14 g, Carbohydrates: 5 g, Fat: 5 g, Fiber: 2 g, Cholesterol: 0 mg, Sodium: 200 mg, Potassium: 300 mg

Chapter 3. Appetizers and Snacks

Crispy Kale Chips

Prep. time: 10 min | Cook time: 15 min | Serves: 4

Ingredients

- 1 large bunch of kale, washed and dried
- 1 tablespoon olive oil
- 1/2 teaspoon sea salt
- Optional seasonings: garlic powder, smoked paprika, or nutritional yeast

Directions

1. Preheat Oven and Prepare Kale: Preheat your oven to 300°F (150°C). Remove the stems and tear the kale leaves into small chunks.
2. Season the Kale: Place the kale pieces in a large bowl. Lightly coat with olive oil and scatter sea salt over the top. Toss to evenly coat. Add any optional seasonings as desired.
3. Arrange on Baking Sheet: Spread the kale evenly on a baking sheet lined with parchment paper, ensuring the leaves don't overlap too much.
4. Bake: Bake in the oven for 15 minutes or until the edges are slightly browned and the leaves are crisp. Turn the leaves halfway through baking to ensure even crisping.
5. Cool and Serve: Remove the kale chips from the oven and let them cool on the baking sheet for a few minutes to crisp them further.

Nutritional Information:
Calories: 58, Protein: 2 g, Carbohydrates: 4 g, Fat: 4 g, Fiber: 1 g, Cholesterol: 0 mg, Sodium: 300 mg, Potassium: 212 mg

Avocado and Tomato Bruschetta

Prep. time: 15 min | Cook time: 5 min (for toasting bread) | Serves: 6

Ingredients

- 1 baguette, sliced into 1/2-inch pieces
- 2 ripe avocados, peeled and diced
- 2 large tomatoes, diced
- 1/4 cup chopped fresh basil
- 2 cloves garlic, minced
- 1 tablespoon balsamic vinegar
- 2 tablespoons olive oil
- Salt and pepper to taste

Directions

1. Toast the Bread: Heat the oven to 400°F (200°C). Arrange the baguette slices on a baking sheet and gently dab each piece with olive oil. Bake for approximately 5 minutes or until they are golden and crisp.
2. Prepare the Topping: In a medium bowl, combine the diced avocados, tomatoes, basil, and minced garlic. Drizzle with balsamic vinegar and the remaining olive oil—season with salt and pepper to taste.
3. Assemble the Bruschetta: Spoon the avocado and tomato mixture onto each toasted baguette slice.
4. Serve Immediately: Arrange the bruschetta on a serving platter and serve immediately to maintain the bread's crispness.

Nutritional Information:
Calories: 250, Protein: 5 g, Carbohydrates: 27 g, Fat: 14 g, Fiber: 5 g, Cholesterol: 0 mg, Sodium: 180 mg, Potassium: 400 mg

Roasted Chickpea Poppers

Prep. time: 10 min | Cook time: 30 min | Serves: 4

Ingredients

- 2 cans (15 oz each) chickpeas, drained, rinsed, and dried
- 2 tablespoons olive oil
- 1 teaspoon smoked paprika
- 1/2 teaspoon garlic powder
- 1/2 teaspoon onion powder
- Salt and black pepper to taste
- Optional: a pinch of cayenne pepper for extra heat

Directions

1. Prepare Chickpeas: Preheat your oven to 400°F (200°C). Ensure chickpeas are thoroughly dried after rinsing to ensure they become crispy when roasted.
2. Season the Chickpeas: In a bowl, toss the chickpeas with olive oil, smoked salt, paprika, onion powder, garlic powder, black pepper, and cayenne pepper if using.
3. Roast: Spread the chickpeas in a single layer on a baking sheet. Roast in the oven for about 30 minutes, shaking the pan occasionally to ensure they roast evenly.
4. Cool and Serve: Take out of the oven and allow to cool briefly. They will become crisper as they cool down.

Nutritional Information:
Calories: 210, Protein: 9 g, Carbohydrates: 28 g, Fat: 8 g, Fiber: 8 g, Cholesterol: 0 mg, Sodium: 300 mg, Potassium: 290 mg

Zucchini and Corn Fritters

Prep. time: 20 min | Cook time: 10 min | Serves: 4

Ingredients

- 2 medium zucchinis, grated
- 1 cup corn kernels (fresh, frozen, or canned)
- 1/2 cup whole wheat flour
- 1/4 cup grated Parmesan cheese (optional)
- 2 green onions, finely chopped
- 1 egg, beaten
- Salt and pepper to taste
- 2 tablespoons olive oil for frying

Directions

1. Prepare the Zucchini: Place the grated zucchini in a colander, sprinkle with salt, and let it sit for 10 minutes. Squeeze out as much moisture as possible.
2. Mix Ingredients: In a large bowl, combine the drained zucchini, corn, flour, Parmesan cheese (if using), green onions, and beaten egg—season with salt and pepper. Stir until the mixture is well combined and holds together.
3. Fritters: Heat the olive oil in a large skillet over medium heat. Scoop a tablespoon of the zucchini mixture into the skillet, flattening it slightly to form a patty. Cook in batches to avoid overcrowding the pan.
4. Cook: Fry each patty on each side for about 4-5 minutes or until golden brown and crispy.
5. Serve: Serve the fritters hot, optionally with a dollop of low-fat yogurt or sour cream and a sprinkle of fresh herbs.

Nutritional Information:
Calories: 180, Protein: 6 g, Carbohydrates: 24 g, Fat: 8 g, Fiber: 3 g, Cholesterol: 50 mg, Sodium: 180 mg, Potassium: 320 mg

Sweet Potato and Beet Chips

Prep. time: 15 min | Cook time: 25 min | Serves: 4

Ingredients

- 1 large sweet potato, thinly sliced
- 1 large beet, thinly sliced
- 2 tablespoons olive oil
- Salt to taste
- Optional: pinch of cayenne pepper or smoked paprika for seasoning

Directions

1. Preheat the Oven: Heat the oven to 375°F (190°C). Cover two sizable baking trays with parchment paper.
2. Prepare Vegetables: Use a mandoline or a sharp knife to slice the sweet potato and beet into skinny slices. The thinner the slices, the crispier your chips will be.
3. Season: Place the vegetable slices in a large bowl. Drizzle with olive oil and toss to coat evenly. Sprinkle with salt and optional seasonings if desired.
4. Arrange on Baking Sheets: Spread the slices in a single layer on the prepared baking sheets, ensuring they don't overlap.
5. Bake: Cook in the oven for 20-25 minutes or until crisp, turning the slices halfway through. Watch closely towards the end to prevent burning.
6. Cool and Serve: Remove the chips from the oven and let them cool on the baking sheets for a few minutes to crisp up further.

Nutritional Information:
Calories: 150, Protein: 2 g, Carbohydrates: 18 g, Fat: 9 g, Fiber: 3 g, Cholesterol: 0 mg, Sodium: 150 mg, Potassium: 400 mg

Edamame and Garlic Dip

Prep. time: 10 min | Cook time: 5 min (if using frozen edamame) | Serves: 4

Ingredients

- 2 cups shelled edamame (fresh or frozen)
- 2 cloves garlic, minced
- 1/4 cup tahini
- 1/4 cup water
- 2 tablespoons olive oil
- Juice of 1 lemon
- Salt and pepper to taste
- Optional: 1 tablespoon chopped fresh cilantro or parsley for garnish

Directions

1. Prepare Edamame: If using frozen edamame, cook according to package instructions, usually boiling in water for about 5 minutes. Drain well.
2. Blend Ingredients: In a food processor, combine the cooked edamame, minced garlic, tahini, water, olive oil, and lemon juice. Blend until smooth.
3. Season: Add salt and pepper as desired. Keep blending until you reach a creamy, smooth consistency.
4. Chill: For the best flavor, chill the dip for at least 30 minutes before serving to allow the flavors to meld.
5. Serve: Garnish with chopped cilantro or parsley if desired. Serve with raw vegetables, whole-grain crackers, or as a spread on sandwiches.

Nutritional Information:
Calories: 220, Protein: 12 g, Carbohydrates: 13 g, Fat: 15 g, Fiber: 5 g, Cholesterol: 0 mg, Sodium: 15 mg, Potassium: 430 mg

Greek Yogurt and Cucumber Gazpacho

Prep. time: 4 min | Cook time: 15 min | Serves: 0

Ingredients

- 2 large cucumbers, peeled, seeded, and chopped
- 1 cup plain Greek yogurt
- 1 clove garlic, minced
- 1 small red onion, chopped
- 1 green bell pepper, seeded and chopped
- 2 tablespoons fresh dill, chopped
- Juice of 1 lemon
- 2 tablespoons olive oil
- Salt and pepper to taste
- 1/2 cup cold water (adjust for desired consistency)
- Optional: diced avocado or croutons for garnish

Directions

1. Blend Ingredients: In a blender or food processor, combine cucumbers, Greek yogurt, garlic, red onion, green bell pepper, dill, lemon juice, and olive oil. Blend until smooth.
2. Adjust Consistency: Add cold water to reach your preferred consistency, blending after each addition until the gazpacho is somewhat fluid yet still slightly thick.
3. Season: Sample and fine-tune the seasoning with salt and pepper as needed. For a tangy flavor, add a bit of lemon juice.
4. Chill: Refrigerate the gazpacho for at least 2 hours to allow the flavors to meld and the soup to chill thoroughly.
5. Serve: Serve cold, garnished with diced avocado or croutons if desired.

Nutritional Information:
Calories: 150, Protein: 8 g, Carbohydrates: 12 g, Fat: 8 g, Fiber: 2 g, Cholesterol: 5 mg, Sodium: 50 mg, Potassium: 400 mg

Tomato and Basil Skewers

Prep. time: 10 min | Cook time: 0 min | Serves: 6

Ingredients

- 24 cherry tomatoes
- 12 fresh basil leaves
- 12 small mozzarella balls (use part-skim for lower cholesterol)
- 2 tablespoons balsamic vinegar
- 2 tablespoons olive oil
- Salt and pepper to taste
- 12 small skewers or toothpicks

Directions

1. Assemble Skewers: Thread each skewer with two cherry tomatoes, one basil leaf folded in half, and one mozzarella ball. Repeat until all ingredients are used.
2. Prepare Dressing: In a small bowl, whisk together balsamic vinegar, olive oil, salt, and pepper.
3. Drizzle and Serve: Arrange the skewers on a platter and drizzle with the balsamic dressing before serving.
4. Optional: For a touch of sweetness, you can reduce the balsamic vinegar by simmering it over low heat until thickened and then drizzle it over the skewers.

Nutritional Information:
Calories: 120, Protein: 6 g, Carbohydrates: 4 g, Fat: 9 g, Fiber: 1 g, Cholesterol: 10 mg, Sodium: 180 mg, Potassium: 150 mg

Chia Seed and Berry Yogurt Parfaits

Prep. time: 15 min | Cook time: 0 min (plus chilling time) | Serves: 4

Ingredients

- 2 cups plain Greek yogurt (low-fat or non-fat for lower cholesterol)
- 4 tablespoons chia seeds
- 2 tablespoons honey or maple syrup (optional)
- 1 cup mixed berries (like strawberries, blueberries, raspberries)
- 1/2 cup granola (choose a low-fat, high-fiber variety)

Directions

1. Mix Yogurt and Chia Seeds: Mix Greek yogurt with chia seeds and honey or maple syrup in a medium bowl. Stir well to combine.
2. Chill: Let the yogurt mixture sit in the refrigerator for at least 1 hour or overnight to allow the chia seeds to swell and thicken the yogurt.
3. Assemble Parfaits: Spoon a layer of the chia yogurt into glasses or parfait dishes, followed by a layer of mixed berries. Repeat the layers until all ingredients are used up, ending with a layer of berries on top.
4. Top with Granola: Just before serving, sprinkle each parfait with granola for added crunch.

Nutritional Information:
Calories: 180, Protein: 12 g, Carbohydrates: 24 g, Fat: 6 g, Fiber: 5 g, Cholesterol: 5 mg, Sodium: 50 mg, Potassium: 250 mg

Fig and Ricotta Crostinis

Prep. time:10 min | Cook time: 5 min | Serves: 4

Ingredients

- 1 baguette, sliced into 12 thin pieces
- 1 cup part-skim ricotta cheese
- 6 fresh figs, sliced
- 2 tablespoons honey
- 1 tablespoon balsamic vinegar
- Fresh thyme leaves for garnish
- Salt and pepper to taste

Directions

1. Toast the Baguette Slices: Preheat your oven to 375°F (190°C). Place the baguette slices on a baking sheet and toast in the oven for about 5 minutes or until golden and crisp.
2. Prepare the Ricotta: Season the ricotta with salt and pepper in a small bowl. Stir well to combine.
3. Assemble the Crostinis: Spread each toasted baguette slice with a generous layer of seasoned ricotta. Top with a few slices of fig.
4. Drizzle and Garnish: Drizzle honey and a little balsamic vinegar over each crostini. Sprinkle with fresh thyme leaves.
5. Serve Immediately: Arrange the crostinis on a serving platter and serve immediately.

Nutritional Information:
Calories: 220, Protein: 10 g, Carbohydrates: 28 g, Fat: 8 g, Fiber: 2 g, Cholesterol: 20 mg, Sodium: 200 mg, Potassium: 120 mg

Stuffed Cherry Tomatoes

Prep. time: 20 min | Cook time: 0 min | Serves: 6

Ingredients

- 24 cherry tomatoes
- 1 cup cottage cheese, low-fat
- 1/4 cup finely chopped green onions
- 1/4 cup finely chopped celery
- 2 tablespoons chopped fresh basil
- 1 clove garlic, minced
- Salt and pepper to taste
- Optional: a sprinkle of paprika for garnish

Directions

1. Prepare Tomatoes: Cut a thin slice off the top of each cherry tomato and scoop out the inside with a small spoon or melon baller. Set the hollowed-out tomatoes aside.
2. Make the Filling: In a mixing bowl, combine the cottage cheese, green onions, celery, basil, and minced garlic—season with salt and pepper to taste.
3. Stuff the Tomatoes: Carefully spoon or pipe the cottage cheese mixture into the hollowed-out tomatoes.
4. Chill: Place the stuffed tomatoes in the refrigerator for at least 30 minutes before serving to allow the flavors to meld.
5. Serve: Arrange the stuffed tomatoes on a platter. Sprinkle with paprika if desired for a bit of color and extra flavor.

Nutritional Information:
Calories: 50, Protein: 6 g, Carbohydrates: 4 g, Fat: 1 g, Fiber: 1 g, Cholesterol: 3 mg, Sodium: 80 mg, Potassium: 150 mg

Chapter 4. Soups and Salads

Lentil and Spinach Soup

Prep. time: 10 min | Cook time: 30 min | Serves: 4

Ingredients

- 1 cup dried green lentils, rinsed
- One tablespoon of olive oil
- 1 large onion, chopped
- 2 garlic cloves, minced
- 1 carrot, diced
- 1 celery stalk, diced
- 6 cups vegetable broth
- 1 teaspoon ground cumin
- 1/2 teaspoon ground coriander
- Salt and pepper to taste
- 2 cups fresh spinach leaves
- 1 tablespoon lemon juice (optional)

Directions

1. Sauté Vegetables: Heat the olive oil in a large pot over medium heat. Add the onion, garlic, carrot, and celery. Sauté until the vegetables are softened, about 5 minutes.
2. Cook Lentils: Add the rinsed lentils, vegetable broth, cumin, and coriander to the pot—season with salt and pepper. Bring to a boil, then reduce heat and simmer, covered, for about 20 minutes or until the lentils are tender.
3. Add Spinach: Stir in the fresh spinach and continue to simmer until it has wilted about 3 minutes.
4. Finish with Lemon: Remove from heat and stir in lemon juice if using for added brightness.
5. Serve: Adjust seasoning if needed, and serve hot.

Nutritional Information:
Calories: 230, Protein: 14 g, Carbohydrates: 38 g, Fat: 4 g, Fiber: 16 g, Cholesterol: 0 mg, Sodium: 300 mg, Potassium: 740 mg

Pumpkin and Coconut Soup

Prep. time: 15 min | Cook time: 30 min | Serves: 4

Ingredients

- 2 tablespoons olive oil
- 1 onion, chopped
- 2 garlic cloves, minced
- 1 tablespoon grated ginger
- 4 cups pumpkin puree (fresh or canned)
- 3 cups vegetable broth
- 1 can (14 oz) coconut milk
- 1 teaspoon curry powder
- Salt and pepper to taste
- Optional: Fresh cilantro or parsley for garnish

Directions

1. Sauté Aromatics: Heat the olive oil in a sizable pot over medium heat. Include the diced onion, crushed garlic, and shredded ginger. Sauté until the onion is translucent, about 5 minutes.
2. Add Pumpkin and Spices: Stir in the pumpkin puree and curry powder. Cook for a couple of minutes to combine the flavors.
3. Simmer: Add the vegetable broth and bring the mixture to a boil. Reduce the heat and simmer for about 20 minutes.
4. Blend and Add Coconut Milk: Use an immersion blender to puree the soup until smooth. Stir in the coconut milk and heat through, careful not to boil—season with salt and pepper.
5. Serve: Ladle the soup into bowls and garnish with fresh cilantro or parsley if desired.

Nutritional Information:
Calories: 280, Protein: 4 g, Carbohydrates: 24 g, Fat: 20 g, Fiber: 6 g, Cholesterol: 0 mg, Sodium: 300 mg, Potassium: 500 mg

Vegetable Soup

Prep. time: 15 min | Cook time: 30 min | Serves: 4

Ingredients

- 1 tablespoon olive oil
- 1 onion, diced
- 2 garlic cloves, minced
- 2 carrots, peeled and diced
- 2 celery stalks, diced
- 1 zucchini, diced
- 1 bell pepper, any color, diced
- 1 cup green beans, trimmed and cut into 1-inch pieces
- 4 cups vegetable broth
- 1 can (14.5 oz) diced tomatoes with juice
- 1 teaspoon dried basil
- 1 teaspoon dried oregano
- Salt and pepper to taste
- Optional: 1 cup chopped kale or spinach

Directions

1. Sauté Vegetables: Heat the olive oil in a large pot over medium heat. Add the onion, garlic, and sauté until the onion becomes translucent, for about 5 minutes.
2. Add More Veggies: Stir in the carrots, celery, zucchini, bell pepper, and green beans. Cook for another 5 minutes, stirring occasionally.
3. Add Liquids and Season: Pour the vegetable broth and diced tomatoes with their juice—season with basil, oregano, salt, and pepper. Bring to a boil.
4. Simmer: Reduce heat and let the soup simmer for about 20 minutes or until the vegetables are tender.
5. Add Greens: If using, add the kale or spinach during the last 5 minutes of cooking.

Nutritional Information:
Calories: 120, Protein: 3 g, Carbohydrates: 23 g, Fat: 3 g, Fiber: 5 g, Cholesterol: 0 mg, Sodium: 480 mg, Potassium: 650 mg

Beetroot and Goat Cheese Arugula Salad

Prep. time: 15 min | Cook time: 0 min (if using pre-cooked beetroots) | Serves: 4

Ingredients

- 4 medium beetroots, cooked, peeled, and sliced
- 4 cups arugula leaves
- 1/2 cup crumbled goat cheese
- 1/4 cup walnuts, chopped
- 2 tablespoons balsamic vinegar
- 1 tablespoon olive oil
- Salt and pepper to taste
- Optional: 1 teaspoon honey or maple syrup for dressing sweetness

Directions

1. Prepare the Salad Base: Arrange the arugula leaves evenly on a large platter or salad bowl.
2. Add Beetroots: Place the sliced beetroots on top of the arugula.
3. Add Goat Cheese and Walnuts: Sprinkle the crumbled goat cheese and chopped walnuts over the beetroots.
4. Dress the Salad: In a small bowl, whisk together the balsamic vinegar, olive oil, salt, pepper, and honey or maple syrup if using. Drizzle the dressing over the salad.
5. Serve: Toss gently to combine before serving or serve as is for guests to mix individually.

Nutritional Information:
Calories: 200, Protein: 6 g, Carbohydrates: 13 g, Fat: 14 g, Fiber: 3 g, Cholesterol: 13 mg, Sodium: 220 mg, Potassium: 400 mg

Carrot and Ginger Puree Soup

Prep. time: 15 min | Cook time: 30 min | Serves: 4

Ingredients

- 1 tablespoon olive oil
- 1 small onion, chopped
- 2 tablespoons fresh ginger, minced
- 1 pound carrots, peeled and sliced
- 4 cups low-sodium vegetable broth
- Salt and pepper to taste Optional garnish: fresh parsley or coriander

Directions

1. Sauté Aromatics: Heat the olive oil in a large pot over medium heat. Add the chopped onion and minced ginger. Cook until the onion is translucent, about 5 minutes.
2. Add Carrots: Stir in the sliced carrots and cook for another 5 minutes, stirring occasionally.
3. Simmer: Add the vegetable broth to the pot. Bring to a boil, then reduce the heat and let it simmer for about 15 minutes or until the carrots are very tender.
4. Puree the Soup: Use an immersion blender to puree the soup until it reaches a creamy consistency. Alternatively, carefully transfer the soup to a blender and process it in batches.
5. Season and Serve: Flavor the soup with salt and pepper as needed. Serve warm, topped with fresh parsley or coriander if preferred.

Nutritional Information:
Calories: 110, Protein: 2 g, Carbohydrates: 19 g, Fat: 4 g, Fiber: 5 g, Cholesterol: 0 mg, Sodium: 300 mg, Potassium: 500 mg

Avocado and Grapefruit Salad with Citrus Vinaigrette

Prep. time: 15 min | Cook time: 0 min) | Serves: 4

Ingredients

- 2 large grapefruits, peeled and sectioned
- 2 avocados, peeled, pitted, and sliced
- 4 cups mixed salad greens (such as arugula and spinach)
- 1/4 red onion, thinly sliced
- 2 tablespoons olive oil
- 2 tablespoons fresh lemon juice
- 1 tablespoon orange juice
- 1 teaspoon honey
- Salt and pepper to taste
- Optional: 2 tablespoons chopped fresh mint or cilantro for garnish

Directions

1. Prepare the salad: Arrange the mixed green salad on a large platter. Top with grapefruit sections, avocado slices, and thinly sliced red onion.
2. Make the Vinaigrette: In a small bowl, whisk together olive oil, lemon juice, orange juice, and honey—season with salt and pepper to taste.
3. Dress the Salad: Drizzle the citrus vinaigrette over the salad just before serving to keep the greens crisp.
4. Garnish and Serve: If desired, sprinkle chopped mint or cilantro over the top for added flavor and freshness.

Nutritional Information:
Calories: 240, Protein: 3 g, Carbohydrates: 20 g, Fat: 18 g, Fiber: 7 g, Cholesterol: 0 mg, Sodium: 20 mg, Potassium: 600 mg

Mediterranean Chickpea Salad with Herbs

Prep. time: 15 min | Cook time: 0 min | Serves: 4

Ingredients

- 2 cans (15 oz each) chickpeas, drained and rinsed
- 1 cucumber, diced
- 1 red bell pepper, diced
- 1/2 red onion, finely chopped
- 1/2 cup cherry tomatoes, halved
- 1/4 cup kalamata olives, pitted and sliced
- 1/4 cup feta cheese, crumbled
- 1/4 cup fresh parsley, chopped
- 1/4 cup fresh mint, chopped
- 3 tablespoons olive oil
- 2 tablespoons lemon juice
- 1 garlic clove, minced
- Salt and pepper to taste

Directions

1.   Mix Salad Components: In a big bowl, mix chickpeas, cucumber, red bell pepper, red onion, cherry tomatoes, olives, feta cheese, parsley, and mint.
2.   Create Dressing: Whisk olive oil, lemon juice, minced garlic, salt, and pepper in a small bowl until smooth.
3.   Coat the Salad: Drizzle the dressing over the salad components and mix thoroughly to ensure an even coating.
4.   Refrigerate and Serve: For optimal taste, refrigerate the salad for at least 30 minutes before serving to let the flavors blend.

Nutritional Information:
Calories: 290, Protein: 10 g, Carbohydrates: 35 g, Fat: 13 g, Fiber: 10 g, Cholesterol: 8 mg, Sodium: 320 mg, Potassium: 360 mg

Tomato Basil Mozzarella Salad

Prep. time: 10 min | Cook time: 0 min | Serves: 4

Ingredients

- 4 large ripe tomatoes, sliced
- 1 ball of fresh mozzarella cheese (8 oz), sliced
- 1/4 cup fresh basil leaves, torn
- 2 tablespoons extra virgin olive oil
- 2 tablespoons balsamic vinegar
- Salt and freshly ground black pepper to taste
- Optional: a pinch of red pepper flakes for a spicy kick

Directions

1.   Arrange the Salad: Alternatively, arrange the sliced tomatoes and mozzarella cheese on a large platter. Sprinkle the torn basil leaves over the top.
2.   Prepare the Dressing: Whisk the olive oil and balsamic vinegar in a small bowl until well combined.
3.   Season: Drizzle the olive oil and vinegar mixture over the tomatoes and mozzarella. Season the salad with salt and black pepper, and add red pepper flakes.
4.   Serve: Let the salad sit for about 5 minutes to allow the flavors to meld before serving.

Nutritional Information:
Calories: 250, Protein: 10 g, Carbohydrates: 7 g, Fat: 20 g, Fiber: 2 g, Cholesterol: 22 mg, Sodium: 180 mg, Potassium: 410 mg

Greek salad with olives

Prep. time: 15 min | Cook time: 0 min | Serves: 4

Ingredients

- 4 medium ripe tomatoes, chopped
- 1 cucumber, peeled and sliced
- 1 red onion, thinly sliced
- 1/2 cup Kalamata olives, pitted
- 1/2 cup feta cheese, crumbled
- 1/4 cup extra virgin olive oil
- 2 tablespoons red wine vinegar
- 1 teaspoon dried oregano
- Salt and pepper to taste
- Optional: 1 green bell pepper, sliced

Directions

1. Combine Vegetables: In a large salad bowl, combine the chopped tomatoes, sliced cucumber, sliced red onion, and optional green bell pepper.
2. Add Olives and Feta: Scatter the Kalamata olives and crumbled feta cheese over the vegetables.
3. Make Dressing: In a small bowl, mix the olive oil, red wine vinegar, dried oregano, salt, and pepper.
4. Dress the Salad: Pour the dressing over the salad and lightly mix to distribute the ingredients uniformly.
5. Serve: Allow the salad to rest for approximately 10 minutes before serving to enable the flavors to blend.

Nutritional Information:
Calories: 250, Protein: 5 g, Carbohydrates: 13 g, Fat: 21 g, Fiber: 3 g, Cholesterol: 25 mg, Sodium: 580 mg, Potassium: 360 mg

Bulgur Wheat and Cucumber Salad

Prep. time: 15 min | Cook time: 10 min | Serves: 4

Ingredients

- 1 cup bulgur wheat
- 2 cups water
- 1 large cucumber, diced
- 1/2 red onion, finely chopped
- 1/4 cup fresh parsley, chopped
- 1/4 cup fresh mint, chopped
- 3 tablespoons olive oil
- 2 tablespoons lemon juice
- Salt and pepper to taste
- Optional: cherry tomatoes or feta cheese for garnish

Directions

1.   Heat the water in a medium saucepan until it boils. Add the bulgur wheat, cover it, and reduce the heat to low. Simmer for about 10 minutes or until the water is absorbed. After turning off the heat, wait five minutes. Using a fork, fluff and let cool.
2.   Combine the cooled bulgur wheat, diced cucumber, red onion, parsley, and mint
3.   in a large salad bowl.
4.   Mix the lemon juice and olive oil in a small bowl—season with salt and pepper.
5.   Toss to combine the salad with the dressing after adding it. Adjust seasoning as needed.
6.   Serve chilled, garnished with cherry tomatoes or crumbled feta cheese if desired.

Nutritional Information:
Calories: 220, Protein: 6g, Carbohydrates: 33g, Fat: 8g, Fiber: 8g, Cholesterol: 0mg, Sodium: 10mg, Potassium: 300mg

Lentil Salad with Roasted Vegetables

Prep. time: 20 min | Cook time: 30 min | Serves: 4

Ingredients

- 1 cup dry green lentils
- 1 small red onion, sliced
- 1 red bell pepper, cut into 1-inch pieces
- 1 zucchini, cut into 1-inch pieces
- 2 carrots, peeled and sliced
- 2 tablespoons olive oil
- Salt and pepper to taste
- 2 tablespoons red wine vinegar
- 1 tablespoon Dijon mustard
- 1 garlic clove, minced
- 1/4 cup fresh parsley, chopped

Directions

1. Preheat oven to 425°F (220°C). After giving the lentils a good rinse, boil them for 15 to 20 minutes or until soft. Drain and set aside.
2. While the lentils cook, toss the red onion, bell pepper, zucchini, and carrots with olive oil, salt, and pepper on a baking sheet. Give the veggies to roast in a preheated oven for 20 minutes or until they are soft and light brown
3. .
4. To make the dressing, combine the red wine vinegar, Dijon mustard, salt, minced garlic, and pepper in a small bowl.
5. Combine the roasted vegetables, cooked lentils, and fresh parsley in a large salad bowl. After pouring the dressing over the salad, toss to ensure an even coating.
6. Adjust the seasoning as necessary, then serve warm or at room temperature.

Nutritional Information:
Calories: 280, Protein: 14g, Carbohydrates: 40g, Fat: 7g, Fiber: 16g, Cholesterol: 0mg, Sodium: 200mg, Potassium: 600mg

Kale Caesar Salad with Almond Croutons

Prep. time: 15 min | Cook time: 10 min | Serves: 4

Ingredients

- 4 cups chopped kale, stems removed
- 1/3 cup sliced almonds
- 1 cup whole wheat bread cubes
- 2 tablespoons olive oil
- 1 clove garlic, minced
- 2 anchovy fillets, finely chopped (optional)
- Juice of 1 lemon
- 1 teaspoon Dijon mustard
- 1 tablespoon finely grated Parmesan cheese plus additional for decoration
- Salt and black pepper to taste

Directions

1. Preheat the oven to 375°F (190°C). To make the croutons, toss the bread cubes with half the olive oil and a pinch of salt. Spread on a baking sheet and bake until golden and crispy, about 10 minutes.
2. Rub the kale with a small amount of olive oil and a pinch of salt to soften the leaves
3. in a large salad bowl.
4. Whisk together the remaining olive oil, lemon juice, minced garlic, Dijon mustard, anchovies, and grated Parmesan cheese in a small bowl to create the dressing.
5. Add the almond croutons and sliced almonds to the kale. Over the salad, drizzle with the dressing and toss to coat the greens.
6. Serve the salad garnished with additional Parmesan cheese and freshly ground black pepper.

Nutritional Information:
220 calories, 8g protein, 18g carbohydrates, 14g fat, 3g fiber, 4mg cholesterol, 340mg sodium, 350mg potassium.

Chapter 5. Fish and Seafood Recipes

Salmon and Spinach Quinoa Salad

Prep. time: 10 min | Cook time: 20 min | Serves: 4

Ingredients

- 1 cup quinoa
- 2 cups water
- 2 salmon fillets (4 oz each)
- 2 cups fresh spinach leaves
- 1/2 cup cherry tomatoes, halved
- 1/4 cup diced cucumber
- 1/4 cup red onion, thinly sliced
- 2 tablespoons olive oil
- 1 lemon, juiced
- Salt and pepper to taste
- Optional: fresh herbs such as dill or parsley for garnish

Directions

1.   Prepare Quinoa: Wash quinoa under cold water. In a medium-sized saucepan, heat 2 cups of water until it boils. Add the quinoa, decrease the heat to low, cover, and let it simmer for 15 minutes or until the water is completely absorbed. Remove it from the stove and let it rest for 5 minutes, then loosen with a fork.
2.   Prepare Salmon: Season salmon fillets with salt and pepper while cooking quinoa. Heat 1 tablespoon of olive oil in a skillet over medium-high heat. Place salmon in the skillet, skin-side down, and cook for 6-7 minutes on each side or until fully cooked. Remove from heat and let cool slightly before flaking into large pieces.
3.   Assemble Salad: In a large bowl, combine cooked quinoa, spinach leaves, cherry tomatoes, cucumber, and red onion. Add flaked salmon.
4.   Dress Salad: Whisk the remaining olive oil and lemon juice in a small bowl. Drizzle over the salad and toss gently to combine—season with salt and pepper to taste.
5.   Serve: Divide the salad among plates and garnish with fresh herbs if desired.

Nutritional Information:
Calories: 320, Protein: 22 g, Carbohydrates: 30 g, Fat: 12 g, Fiber: 5 g, Cholesterol: 50 mg, Sodium: 70 mg, Potassium: 780 mg

Simple Grilled Salmon with Lemon Pepper

Prep. time: 10 min | Cook time: 5 min | Serves: 4

Ingredients

- 4 salmon fillets (6 oz each)
- 2 tablespoons olive oil
- 2 teaspoons lemon pepper seasoning
- 1 lemon, sliced (for garnish)
- Fresh herbs (like dill or parsley) for garnish

Directions

1.   Preheat Grill: Heat your grill to medium-high heat.
2.   Prepare Salmon: Brush each salmon fillet with olive oil and sprinkle evenly with lemon pepper seasoning.
3.   Grill Salmon: Place salmon on the grill, skin side down, and cook for 5-6 minutes. Flip carefully and cook for 4-5 minutes until the salmon is opaque and flakes easily with a fork.
4.   Garnish and Serve: Transfer the grilled salmon to plates. Garnish with fresh lemon slices and a sprinkle of fresh herbs.

Nutritional Information:
Calories: 280, Protein: 34 g, Carbohydrates: 1 g, Fat: 15 g, Fiber: 0 g, Cholesterol: 90 mg, Sodium: 170 mg, Potassium: 840 mg

Tuna Salad with Avocado

Prep. time: 10 min | Cook time: 0 min | Serves: 4

Ingredients

- 2 cans (5 oz each) of tuna in water, drained
- 1 ripe avocado, peeled, pitted, and diced
- 1/2 red onion, finely chopped
- 1/2 cup cherry tomatoes, halved
- 1/4 cup chopped fresh cilantro
- Juice of 1 lime
- 2 tablespoons olive oil
- Salt and pepper to taste
- Optional: 1 small jalapeño, seeded and minced for extra spice

Directions

1. Mix Tuna and Vegetables: In a large bowl, combine the drained tuna, diced avocado, chopped red onion, cherry tomatoes, and cilantro. If using jalapeño, add it to the mix.
2. Dress the Salad: Add the lime juice and olive oil to the tuna mixture. Gently toss to combine all ingredients thoroughly without breaking the avocado too much.
3. Season: Season with salt and pepper according to taste. Adjust the lime juice or olive oil if needed.
4. Chill and Serve: For best flavor, let the salad chill in the refrigerator for 30 minutes before serving. This allows the flavors to meld together nicely.

Nutritional Information:
Calories: 220, Protein: 23 g, Carbohydrates: 8 g, Fat: 12 g, Fiber: 4 g, Cholesterol: 30 mg, Sodium: 210 mg, Potassium: 400 mg

Lemon Garlic Shrimp over Whole-Wheat Pasta

Prep. time: 10 min | Cook time: 0 min | Serves: 4

Ingredients

- 12 oz whole-wheat spaghetti or linguine
- 1 lb large shrimp, peeled and deveined
- 3 tablespoons olive oil
- 4 garlic cloves, minced
- Zest and juice of 1 lemon
- 1/4 teaspoon red pepper flakes (optional)
- 1/4 cup chopped fresh parsley
- Salt and pepper to taste
- Grated Parmesan cheese for serving (optional)

Directions

1. Prepare Pasta: Prepare the whole-wheat pasta as per the instructions on the package until it is firm enough to bite. Drain and set aside, saving 1 cup of the pasta water.
2. Cook Shrimp: Warm the olive oil in a large skillet over medium heat while cooking pasta. Add garlic and red pepper flakes if desired, and sauté for 1 minute until aromatic. Place the shrimp in the skillet and sauté on each side for 2-3 minutes until they are pink and fully cooked. Remove from heat.
3. Combine Shrimp and Pasta: Add the cooked pasta to the skillet with the shrimp. Add the lemon zest, lemon juice, and chopped parsley. Toss to combine, adding a little reserved pasta water if the mixture seems dry—season with salt and pepper to taste.
4. Serve: Divide the pasta among plates and sprinkle with grated Parmesan cheese if desired.

Nutritional Information:
Calories: 410, Protein: 35 g, Carbohydrates: 52 g, Fat: 10 g, Fiber: 8 g, Cholesterol: 185 mg, Sodium: 320 mg, Potassium: 370 mg

Mediterranean Tuna and Olive Salad

Prep. time: 15 min | Cook time: 0 min | Serves: 4

Ingredients

- 2 cans (5 oz each) tuna in olive oil, drained
- 1 cup cherry tomatoes, halved
- 1/2 cup Kalamata olives, pitted and halved
- 1 small red onion, thinly sliced
- 1 cucumber, diced
- 1/4 cup chopped fresh parsley
- 1/4 cup chopped fresh basil
- Juice of 1 lemon
- 2 tablespoons extra virgin olive oil
- Salt and pepper to taste
- Optional: 1 tablespoon capers for extra tang

Directions

1. Combine Ingredients: In a large mixing bowl, combine the drained tuna, cherry tomatoes, Kalamata olives, red onion, cucumber, parsley, and basil. If using, add capers.
2. Dress the salad: Drizzle it with lemon juice and olive oil—season with salt and pepper. Toss everything gently to mix well without breaking the tuna too much.
3. Chill: Cover and chill the salad in the refrigerator for at least 30 minutes for the best flavor to allow the flavors to meld.
4. Serve: Serve the salad chilled, perfect as a standalone meal or accompanied by crusty whole-grain bread.

Nutritional Information:
Calories: 220, Protein: 25 g, Carbohydrates: 8 g, Fat: 11 g, Fiber: 2 g, Cholesterol: 30 mg, Sodium: 580 mg, Potassium: 300 mg

Pesto Grilled Shrimp with Summer Squash

Prep. time: 20 min | Cook time: 10 min | Serves: 4

Ingredients

- 1 pound large shrimp, peeled and deveined
- 2 medium summer squash, sliced into half-inch rounds
- 1/4 cup homemade or store-bought pesto
- 2 tablespoons olive oil
- Salt and pepper to taste
- Lemon wedges for serving

Directions

1. Prep Shrimp and Squash: In a large bowl, combine shrimp, summer squash, pesto, and olive oil. Mix thoroughly to distribute the coating evenly, and season with salt and pepper.
2. Heat Grill: Warm your grill to medium-high heat.
3. Grill Shrimp and Squash: Thread the shrimp and squash onto skewers. Grill for 2-3 minutes per side or until the shrimp are opaque and the squash is tender and has grill marks.
4. Serve: Remove from grill and serve hot with lemon wedges on the side.

Nutritional Information:
Calories: 250, Protein: 24 g, Carbohydrates: 8 g, Fat: 14 g, Fiber: 2 g, Cholesterol: 180 mg, Sodium: 340 mg, Potassium: 300 mg

Lime and Cumin Swordfish Steaks

Prep. time: 15 min | Cook time: 10 min | Serves: 4

Ingredients

- 4 swordfish steaks (about 6 ounces each)
- 2 tablespoons olive oil
- Juice and zest of 2 limes
- 2 teaspoons ground cumin
- 1 teaspoon garlic powder
- Salt and pepper to taste
- Fresh cilantro, chopped (for garnish)

Directions

1.   Marinate the Fish: In a small bowl, mix the olive oil, lime juice, lime zest, cumin, garlic powder, salt, and pepper. Position the swordfish steaks in a shallow dish and drizzle the marinade over them. Cover and chill for at least 30 minutes to let the flavors fuse.
2.   Warm Up the Grill: Set your grill to medium-high heat.
3.   Grill the Steaks: Remove the swordfish from the marinade, letting excess drip off. Grill the steaks for about 5 minutes on each side or until the fish is opaque and flakes easily with a fork.
4.   Serve: Plate the grilled swordfish, garnishing each steak with chopped cilantro.

Nutritional Information:
Calories: 280, Protein: 30 g, Carbohydrates: 2 g, Fat: 17 g, Fiber: 0 g, Cholesterol: 85 mg, Sodium: 125 mg, Potassium: 600 mg

Quick Broiled Scallops with Garlic

Prep. time: 10 min | Cook time: 6 min | Serves: 4

Ingredients

- 1 pound sea scallops, rinsed and patted dry
- 2 tablespoons olive oil
- 3 cloves garlic, minced
- Juice of 1 lemon
- Salt and pepper to taste
- Fresh parsley, chopped (for garnish)

Directions

1.   Preheat the Broiler: Set your oven's broiler to high and place the oven rack about 6 inches from the heat source.
2.   Prepare the Scallops: In a mixing bowl, toss the scallops with olive oil, minced garlic, lemon juice, salt, and pepper until evenly coated.
3.   Arrange the Scallops: Lay the scallops out in a single layer on a baking sheet or broiling pan.
4.   Broil: Place the scallops under the broiler and cook for about 3 minutes on each side until they are opaque and lightly golden.
5.   Serve: Garnish the broiled scallops with fresh parsley and serve immediately.

Nutritional Information:
Calories: 190, Protein: 20 g, Carbohydrates: 5 g, Fat: 10 g, Fiber: 0 g, Cholesterol: 37 mg, Sodium: 560 mg, Potassium: 360 mg

Light & Crispy Baked Clams

Prep. time: 10 min | Cook time: 6 min | Serves: 4

Ingredients

- 1 pound sea scallops, rinsed and patted dry
- 2 tablespoons olive oil
- 3 cloves garlic, minced
- Juice of 1 lemon
- Salt and pepper to taste
- Fresh parsley, chopped (for garnish)

Directions

1. Preheat the Broiler: Set your oven's broiler to high and place the oven rack about 6 inches from the heat source.
2. Prepare the Scallops: In a mixing bowl, toss the scallops with olive oil, minced garlic, lemon juice, salt, and pepper until evenly coated.
3. Arrange the Scallops: Lay the scallops out in a single layer on a baking sheet or broiling pan.
4. Broil: Place the scallops under the broiler and cook for about 3 minutes on each side until they are opaque and lightly golden.
5. Serve: Garnish the broiled scallops with fresh parsley and serve immediately.

Nutritional Information:
Calories: 190, Protein: 20 g, Carbohydrates: 5 g, Fat: 10 g, Fiber: 0 g, Cholesterol: 37 mg, Sodium: 560 mg, Potassium: 360 mg

Honey Garlic Baked Trout

Prep. time: 10 min | Cook time: 15 min | Serves: 4

Ingredients

- 4 trout fillets (about 6 ounces each)
- 3 tablespoons honey
- 2 tablespoons soy sauce (low sodium)
- 1 tablespoon olive oil
- 3 cloves garlic, minced
- Juice of 1 lemon
- Salt and pepper to taste
- Fresh parsley, chopped (for garnish)
- Lemon slices (for garnish)

Directions

1. Prepare Marinade: In a small bowl, whisk together honey, soy sauce, olive oil, garlic, and lemon juice—season with a pinch of salt and pepper.
2. Marinate Trout: Place the trout fillets in a shallow dish or a sealable plastic bag. Pour the marinade over the trout, coating each fillet well. Let the trout marinate in the refrigerator for at least 30 minutes.
3. Preheat Oven: Preheat your oven to 400°F (200°C).
4. Bake Trout: Remove the trout from the marinade and place the fillets skin side down on a baking sheet lined with parchment paper. Bake in the preheated oven for about 12-15 minutes or until the fish flakes easily with a fork.
5. Serve: Garnish baked trout with chopped parsley and lemon slices. Serve immediately.

Nutritional Information:
Calories: 290, Protein: 25 g, Carbohydrates: 18 g, Fat: 12 g, Fiber: 0 g, Cholesterol: 70 mg, Sodium: 240 mg, Potassium: 600 mg

Foil-Baked Flounder with Herbs

Prep. time: 10 min | Cook time: 20 min | Serves: 4

Ingredients

- 4 flounder fillets (about 6 ounces each)
- 2 tablespoons olive oil
- 1 lemon, thinly sliced
- 4 cloves garlic, minced
- 2 tablespoons fresh parsley, chopped
- 2 tablespoons fresh dill, chopped
- Salt and pepper to taste
- Additional herbs like thyme or basil, if desired

Directions

1. Preheat Oven: Preheat your oven to 375°F (190°C).
2. Prepare Foil Packets: Cut four sheets of aluminum foil, large enough to wrap each fillet completely. Place a flounder fillet in the center of each sheet.
3. Season Fillets: Drizzle each fillet with olive oil. Top with minced garlic, a sprinkle of chopped parsley, dill, and additional herbs if using—season with salt and pepper. Place a few lemon slices on top of each fillet.
4. Wrap and Bake: Fold the foil over the fish, sealing the edges tightly to create a packet. Place the foil packets on a baking tray.
5. Bake: Bake in the oven for 15-20 minutes or until the fish is opaque and flakes easily with a fork.

Nutritional Information:
Calories: 210, Protein: 25 g, Carbohydrates: 3 g, Fat: 11 g, Fiber: 1 g, Cholesterol: 55 mg, Sodium: 125 mg, Potassium: 480 mg

Baked Tilapia with Roasted Vegetables

Prep. time: 15 min | Cook time: 25 min | Serves: 4

Ingredients

- 4 tilapia fillets (about 6 ounces each)
- 2 tablespoons olive oil
- 1 teaspoon garlic powder
- 1 teaspoon dried basil
- Salt and pepper to taste
- 1 zucchini, sliced into rounds
- 1 bell pepper, sliced into strips
- 1 small red onion, sliced
- 1 cup cherry tomatoes

Directions

1. Preheat Oven and Prepare Vegetables: Preheat your oven to 400°F (200°C). Toss zucchini, bell pepper, red onion, and cherry tomatoes with 1 tablespoon of olive oil, salt, and pepper. Spread them out on a baking sheet.
2. Season Tilapia: Brush tilapia fillets with the remaining olive oil and season with garlic powder, dried basil, salt, and pepper.
3. Arrange Tilapia with Vegetables: Place the seasoned tilapia fillets among the vegetables on the baking sheet.
4. Bake: Place the baking sheet in the oven and bake for about 20-25 minutes, or until the vegetables are tender and the tilapia flakes easily with a fork.
5. Serve: Remove from oven and serve immediately, garnishing with fresh herbs if desired.

Nutritional Information:
Calories: 230, Protein: 28 g, Carbohydrates: 9 g, Fat: 10 g, Fiber: 2 g, Cholesterol: 85 mg, Sodium: 125 mg, Potassium: 600 mg

Chapter 6. Meat dishes

6.1. Poultry Dishes

Herb-Roasted Chicken Breast

Prep. time: 10 min | Cook time: 25 min | Serves: 4

Ingredients

- 4 boneless, skinless chicken breasts (about 6 ounces each)
- 2 tablespoons olive oil
- 1 teaspoon dried rosemary
- 1 teaspoon dried thyme
- 1/2 teaspoon dried oregano
- 2 cloves garlic, minced
- Salt and pepper to taste
- Lemon wedges for serving

Directions

1. Heat Oven: Warm your oven to 375°F (190°C).
2. Season Chicken: In a small bowl, mix olive oil, rosemary, thyme, oregano, and minced garlic. Rub this mixture well into the chicken breasts and generously sprinkle with salt and pepper.
3. Arrange on Baking Sheet: Place the seasoned chicken breasts on a baking sheet lined with parchment paper.
4. Roast: Bake in the oven for about 25 minutes or until the chicken is cooked and the internal temperature reaches 165°F (74°C).
5. Serve: Let the chicken rest for a few minutes before slicing. Serve with lemon wedges on the side.

Nutritional Information:
Calories: 220, Protein: 35 g, Carbohydrates: 1 g, Fat: 9 g, Fiber: 0 g, Cholesterol: 85 mg, Sodium: 125 mg, Potassium: 400 mg

Garlic Lime Chicken Tenders

Prep. time: 15 min | Cook time: 10 min | Serves: 4

Ingredients

- 1 pound chicken tenders
- 3 tablespoons olive oil
- Juice and zest of 2 limes
- 4 cloves garlic, minced
- 1 teaspoon honey
- 1/2 teaspoon chili powder
- Salt and pepper to taste
- Fresh cilantro, chopped (for garnish)

Directions

1. Marinate the Chicken: In a bowl, whisk together olive oil, lime juice, zest, minced garlic, honey, chili powder, salt, and pepper. Add the chicken tenders, ensuring they are well coated with the marinade. Cover and refrigerate for at least 30 minutes or up to 4 hours.
2. Preheat Grill or Skillet: Heat a grill or a skillet over medium-high heat. If using a skillet, add extra olive oil to prevent sticking.
3. Cook the Chicken: Remove chicken from the marinade, letting excess drip off. Grill or cook in the skillet for 4-5 minutes on each side until the chicken is golden, charred in spots, and cooked through.
4. Garnish and Serve: Sprinkle chopped cilantro over the cooked chicken tenders before serving.

Nutritional Information:
Calories: 210, Protein: 24 g, Carbohydrates: 4 g, Fat: 11 g, Fiber: 0 g, Cholesterol: 65 mg, Sodium: 150 mg, Potassium: 300 mg

Balsamic Glazed Chicken Drumsticks

Prep. time: 10 min | Cook time: 40 min | Serves: 4

Ingredients

- eight chicken drumsticks, skin removed
- 1/4 cup balsamic vinegar
- 2 tablespoons olive oil
- 2 tablespoons honey
- 2 cloves garlic, minced
- 1 teaspoon dried rosemary
- salt and pepper to taste

Directions

1. Preheat Oven: Heat your oven to 375°F (190°C) before use.
2. Prepare the Glaze: In a tiny bowl, combine the balsamic vinegar, olive oil, honey, minced garlic, and dried rosemary—season with salt and pepper.
3. Marinate: Arrange the chicken drumsticks in a baking dish and pour the glaze over them, turning to coat evenly. Let marinate for at least 20 minutes in the refrigerator.
4. Bake: Remove the chicken from the refrigerator and bake in the oven for 40 minutes until it is cooked and the glaze is caramelized. Halfway through cooking, moisten the chicken with the juices from the pan.
5. Serve: Serve the drumsticks hot, drizzled with any remaining glaze from the baking dish.

Nutritional Information:
Calories: 290, Protein: 27 g, Carbohydrates: 15 g, Fat: 13 g, Fiber: 0 g, Cholesterol: 120 mg, Sodium: 320 mg, Potassium: 370 mg

Spiced Orange Chicken Skewers

Prep. time: 20 min | Cook time: 10 min | Serves: 4

Ingredients

- 1 pound of boneless, cube-sized, skinless chicken breasts
- 1/4 cup fresh orange juice
- 2 tablespoons olive oil
- 1 tablespoon honey
- 1 teaspoon ground cumin
- 1/2 teaspoon paprika
- 1/4 teaspoon ground cinnamon
- Zest of 1 orange
- Salt and pepper to taste
- Wooden or metal skewers

Directions

1. Marinate the Chicken: In a bowl, whisk together orange juice, olive oil, honey, cumin, paprika, cinnamon, orange zest, salt, and pepper. Mix to coat after adding the chicken cubes. Cover and chill in the refrigerator to marinate for at least 2 hours, ideally all night.
2. Preheat Grill: Preheat your grill or grill pan to medium-high heat. Suppose using wooden skewers, immerse them in water for at least 30 minutes before grilling to avoid charring.
3. Assemble Skewers: Thread the marinated chicken cubes onto skewers.
4. Grill: Grill the skewers on each side for 4-5 minutes or until the chicken is thoroughly cooked and has excellent grill marks.
5. Serve: Serve the chicken skewers hot, garnished with additional fresh herbs or orange zest if desired.

Nutritional Information:
Calories: 230, Protein: 26 g, Carbohydrates: 10 g, Fat: 10 g, Fiber: 1 g, Cholesterol: 65 mg, Sodium: 150 mg, Potassium: 300 mg

Rosemary Lemon Roast Turkey

Prep. time: 20 min | Cook time: 3 hours | Serves: 6

Ingredients

- 1 whole turkey (about 12 pounds), thawed and giblets removed
- 4 tablespoons olive oil
- 2 lemons, halved
- Four sprigs of fresh rosemary
- 4 garlic cloves, minced
- Salt and pepper to taste

Directions

1. Preheat Oven: Preheat your oven to 325°F (165°C).
2. Prepare the Turkey: Pat the turkey dry with paper towels. Rub the skin and cavity with olive oil. Lavishly season the interior and exterior with salt and pepper. Stuff the cavity with lemon halves, rosemary sprigs, and minced garlic.
3. Roast Turkey: Place the turkey breast on a roasting pan rack. Cover loosely with aluminum foil to avoid over-browning. Cook in the preheated oven, occasionally moistening with juices from the pan. After 2 hours, remove the foil and roast for approximately another hour, or until a meat thermometer in the deepest section of the thigh shows 165°F (74°C).
4. Rest Before Serving: Remove the turkey from the oven, drape it with foil, and let it rest for twenty minutes before slicing. This process helps the juices spread evenly through the meat, ensuring it stays succulent and tasty.
5. Serve: Cut the turkey into slices and serve with your favorite sides.

Nutritional Information:

Calories: 320, Protein: 48 g, Carbohydrates: 2 g, Fat: 12 g, Fiber: 0 g, Cholesterol: 125 mg, Sodium: 200 mg, Potassium: 500 mg

Zesty Italian Chicken Meatballs

Prep. time: 15 min | Cook time: 20 min | Serves: 4

Ingredients

- 1 pound ground chicken
- 1/4 cup breadcrumbs
- 1/4 cup grated Parmesan cheese
- 1 large egg
- 2 cloves garlic, minced
- 2 tablespoons fresh parsley, chopped
- 1 teaspoon dried oregano
- 1/2 teaspoon red pepper flakes
- Salt and pepper to taste
- 1/2 cup low-sodium marinara sauce

Directions

1. Preheat Oven: Preheat your oven to 400°F (200°C).
2. Mix Ingredients: In a large bowl, combine the ground chicken, breadcrumbs, Parmesan cheese, egg, garlic, parsley, oregano, red pepper flakes, salt, and pepper. Mix well until everything is evenly distributed.
3. Form Meatballs: Form the mixture into 1-inch meatballs and place on a parchment paper-lined baking pan.
4. Bake: In the oven for 15-20 minutes or until the meatballs are cooked and golden outside.
5. Serve with Sauce: Warm the marinara sauce in a saucepan over medium heat. Add the baked meatballs to the sauce and gently toss to coat.

Nutritional Information:

Calories: 230, Protein: 27 g, Carbohydrates: 9 g, Fat: 10 g, Fiber: 1 g, Cholesterol: 140 mg, Sodium: 320 mg, Potassium: 370 mg

Asian Sesame Chicken Salad

Prep. time: 20 min | Cook time: 10 min | Serves: 4

Ingredients

- 2 boneless, skinless chicken breasts
- 6 cups mixed salad greens (like romaine, arugula, and radicchio)
- 1 cup shredded carrots
- 1 red bell pepper, thinly sliced
- 1/2 cup sliced almonds, toasted
- 2 tablespoons sesame seeds
- 1/4 cup cilantro, chopped
- For the dressing:
- 1/4 cup soy sauce (low sodium)
- 2 tablespoons sesame oil
- 1 tablespoon rice vinegar
- 2 tablespoons honey
- 1 teaspoon fresh ginger, grated
- 1 clove garlic, minced

Directions

1. Cook Chicken: Season the chicken breasts lightly with salt and pepper. Grill or pan-fry over medium heat until cooked, about 5 minutes per side. Let cool, and then slice thinly.
2. Prepare Salad: In a large bowl, combine the salad greens, shredded carrots, sliced red bell pepper, and chopped cilantro.
3. Make Dressing: In a small bowl, whisk together soy sauce, sesame oil, rice vinegar, honey, grated ginger, and minced garlic.
4. Toss Salad: Add the sliced chicken to the salad greens mixture. After adding the dressing, stir to ensure it is evenly distributed. Sprinkle toasted almonds and sesame seeds over the Top.
5. Serve: Divide the salad among plates and serve immediately.

Nutritional Information:
Calories: 290, Protein: 28 g, Carbohydrates: 18 g, Fat: 12 g, Fiber: 4 g, Cholesterol: 60 mg, Sodium: 320 mg, Potassium: 650 mg

Greek Yogurt Marinated Chicken Kabobs

Prep. time: 20 min (plus marinating time) | Cook time: 10 min | Serves: 4

Ingredients

- 1 pound chicken breast, cut into 1-inch cubes
- 1 cup plain Greek yogurt
- 2 cloves garlic, minced
- Juice of 1 lemon
- 2 teaspoons dried oregano
- 1/2 teaspoon paprika
- Salt and pepper to taste
- 1 red onion, cut into chunks
- 1 bell pepper, cut into chunks
- 8 wooden or metal skewers

Directions

1. Marinate Chicken: In a bowl, mix the Greek yogurt, garlic, lemon juice, oregano, paprika, salt, and pepper. Add the chicken cubes and coat them thoroughly with the marinade. Cover and refrigerate for at least 2 hours, preferably overnight.
2. Preheat Grill: Heat your grill to medium-high heat. If you use wooden skewers, immerse them in water for at least 30 minutes before use to avoid charring.
3. Assemble Kabobs: Thread the marinated chicken, onion, and bell pepper alternately onto the skewers.
4. Grill Kabobs: Grill them for ten to twelve minutes, rotating them occasionally or until the chicken is cooked. It has excellent grill marks.
5. Serve: Serve the kabobs hot, optionally with a side of tzatziki sauce or a fresh salad.

Nutritional Information:

Calories: 180, Protein: 28 g, Carbohydrates: 9 g, Fat: 3 g, Fiber: 2 g, Cholesterol: 65 mg, Sodium: 150 mg, Potassium: 450 mg

Chicken and Vegetable Soup

Prep. time: 15 min | Cook time: 30 min | Serves: 4

Ingredients

- 2 boneless, skinless chicken breasts, diced
- 1 tablespoon olive oil
- 1 onion, chopped
- 2 carrots, sliced
- 2 celery stalks, sliced
- 3 cloves garlic, minced
- 6 cups low-sodium chicken broth
- 1 cup green beans, trimmed and cut into 1-inch pieces
- 1/2 cup frozen peas
- 1 teaspoon dried thyme
- Salt and pepper to taste
- Fresh parsley, chopped for garnish

Directions

1. Sauté Vegetables: Heat the olive oil over medium heat in a large pot. Add the onion, carrots, and celery. Cook until the vegetables begin to tenderize, approximately 5 minutes. Add the garlic and cook for one more minute.
2. Prepare Chicken: Place the chopped chicken into the pot and cook until it is thoroughly white roughly 5-7 minutes.
3. Add Broth and Simmer: Add the chicken broth and heat the mixture until it boils. Lower the temperature to low and permit it to simmer for 15 minutes.
4. Add Remaining Vegetables: Stir in the green beans, peas, and dried thyme. Season with salt and pepper. Simmer for another 10 minutes or until all the vegetables are tender.
5. Serve: Spoon the soup into bowls, top with fresh parsley, and serve warm.

Nutritional Information:

Calories: 220, Protein: 26 g, Carbohydrates: 15 g, Fat: 6 g, Fiber: 4 g, Cholesterol: 55 mg, Sodium: 320 mg, Potassium: 650 mg

Turkey and Spinach Meatballs

Prep. time: 15 min | Cook time: 20 min | Serves: 4

Ingredients

- 1 pound ground turkey breast
- 1 cup fresh spinach, finely chopped
- 1/4 cup whole wheat breadcrumbs
- 1/4 cup grated Parmesan cheese
- 1 egg white
- 2 cloves garlic, minced
- 1 teaspoon dried oregano
- 1/2 teaspoon salt
- 1/4 teaspoon black pepper
- Olive oil spray

Directions

1. Preheat the Oven: Set the oven to 375°F (190°C). Drizzle some olive oil on a baking pan covered with parchment paper.
2. Ingredients: Combine ground turkey, chopped spinach, breadcrumbs, Parmesan, egg, oregano, garlic, salt, and pepper in a large bowl. Blend the components well.
3. Shape Meatballs: Using the ingredients, roll 1-inch meatballs and arrange them on the preheated baking sheet.
4. Bake: In the oven for 20 minutes or until the meatballs are cooked and lightly golden outside.
5. Serve: Serve the meatballs hot, with marinara sauce if desired, or incorporate into your favorite pasta dish.

Nutritional Information:
Calories: 190, Protein: 28 g, Carbohydrates: 6 g, Fat: 6 g, Fiber: 1 g, Cholesterol: 90 mg, Sodium: 450 mg, Potassium: 300 mg

One-Pot Chicken and Broccoli Pasta

Prep. time: 10 min | Cook time: 20 min | Serves: 4

Ingredients

- 2 boneless, skinless chicken breasts, diced
- 2 cups broccoli florets
- 8 ounces whole wheat penne pasta
- 2 cloves garlic, minced
- 1 onion, chopped
- 3 cups low-sodium chicken broth
- 1 cup skim milk
- 1 teaspoon olive oil
- 1/2 teaspoon salt
- 1/4 teaspoon blackpepper
- 1/4 cup grated Parmesan
- Optional: Red pepper flakes for added spice

Directions

1. Sauté Chicken and Vegetables: Heat the olive oil over medium heat in a large pot. Add the diced chicken, chopped onion, and minced garlic. Cook until the chicken is browned, and the onion is translucent about 5-7 minutes.
2. Add Pasta and Liquids: Add the whole wheat penne, chicken broth, and milk to the pot. After bringing it to a boil, lower the heat to a simmer. Let cook for 10 minutes, stirring occasionally.
3. Incorporate Broccoli: Add the broccoli florets to the pot. Continue to cook for another 5 minutes or until the pasta is al dente and the broccoli is tender.
4. Finish and Serve: Stir in the grated Parmesan cheese and season with salt and pepper. If you like it a little hotter, add some red pepper flakes. Serve hot.

Nutritional Information:
Calories: 350, Protein: 28 g, Carbohydrates: 44 g, Fat: 7 g, Fiber: 6 g, Cholesterol: 55 mg, Sodium: 430 mg, Potassium: 500 mg

Turkey and Zucchini Skillet

Prep. time: 10 min | Cook time: 20 min | Serves: 4

Ingredients

- 1 pound ground turkey breast
- 2 medium zucchinis, diced
- 1 bell pepper, diced
- 1 onion, chopped
- 2 cloves garlic, minced
- 1 tablespoon olive oil
- 1 teaspoon dried oregano
- 1/2 teaspoon salt
- 1/4 teaspoon black pepper
- 1/4 cup low-sodium chicken broth
- 1 tablespoon tomato paste

Directions

1. Heat Oil and Sauté Vegetables: Heat olive oil over medium heat in a large skillet. Add the chopped onion, minced garlic, and diced bell pepper. Simmer for approximately five minutes or until the veggies are tender.
2. Cook Turkey: Add the ground turkey to the skillet. Break it up with a spoon and cook until it is no longer pink about 8 minutes.
3. Add Zucchini: Stir in the diced zucchini, dried oregano, salt, and black pepper. Cook for another 5 minutes until the zucchini is tender.
4. Mix in Broth and Tomato Paste: Add the tomato paste and chicken broth to the skillet. Stir well to combine all the ingredients—cook for two more minutes to allow the flavors to mingle.
5. Serve: Remove the skillet from the burner and serve the hot turkey and zucchini mixture. If desired, garnish with fresh herbs.

Nutritional Information:
Calories: 240, Protein: 27 g, Carbohydrates: 10 g, Fat: 10 g, Fiber: 2 g, Cholesterol: 60 mg, Sodium: 320 mg, Potassium: 650 mg

6.2. Beef and Pork

Grilled Pork Tenderloin with Herbs

Prep. time: 15 min | Cook time: 25 min | Serves: 4

Ingredients

- 1 pork tenderloin (about 1 pound)
- 2 cloves garlic, minced
- 2 tablespoons fresh rosemary, finely chopped
- 2 tablespoons fresh thyme, finely chopped
- 1 tablespoon olive oil
- Salt and pepper, to taste

Directions

1. Mix the garlic, rosemary, thyme, and olive oil in a small bowl. Season the pork tenderloin with salt and pepper, then apply the herb mixture evenly over the entire pork.
2. Preheat the grill to medium-high heat. Once it hot, place the pork tenderloin on the grill.
3. Grill the pork for about 12-15 minutes on each side, turning occasionally, until the internal temperature reaches 145°F (63°C).
4. Remove the pork from the grill and let it rest for 5 minutes before slicing.
5. Serve the sliced pork tenderloin alongside a portion of grilled vegetables or a fresh salad.

Nutritional Information:
200 calories, 25g protein, 2g carbohydrates, 10g fat, 0g fiber, 70mg cholesterol, 65mg sodium, 400mg potassium.

Pork and Vegetable Stir-Fry

Prep. time: 20 min | Cook time: 15 min | Serves: 4

Ingredients

- 1 pound pork tenderloin, thinly sliced
- 1 bell pepper, julienned
- 1 carrot, thinly sliced
- 1 small zucchini, sliced
- 1 onion, sliced
- 2 cloves garlic, minced
- 2 tablespoons soy sauce (low sodium)
- 1 tablespoon olive oil
- 1 teaspoon ginger, grated
- Salt and pepper to taste
- Optional: sesame seeds for garnish

Directions

1. Heat the olive oil in a large skillet or wok over medium-high heat. Add the garlic and ginger, sautéing for about 30 seconds until fragrant.
2. Add the pork slices to the skillet and stir-fry until they start to brown, about 3-4 minutes.
3. Introduce the bell pepper, carrot, zucchini, and onion to the skillet. Continue to stir-fry for another 7-10 minutes until the vegetables are tender and the pork is fully cooked.
4. Mix in the soy sauce, then season with salt and pepper.Cook for an extra 2 minutes to allow the flavors to combine.
5. Serve warm, garnished with sesame seeds if preferred.

Nutritional Information:
220 calories, 27g protein, 10g carbohydrates, 7g fat, 3g fiber, 60mg cholesterol, 450mg sodium, 650mg potassium.

Balsamic Glazed Pork Chops

Prep. time: 10 min | Cook time: 20 min | Serves: 4

Ingredients

- 4 boneless pork chops, about 1-inch thick
- 1/4 cup balsamic vinegar
- 2 tablespoons honey
- 1 tablespoon Dijon mustard
- 2 cloves garlic, minced
- Salt and freshly ground black pepper to taste
- 1 tablespoon olive oil

Directions

1. In a small bowl, whisk together balsamic vinegar, honey, Dijon mustard, and garlic.
2. Season pork chops with salt and pepper. Warm olive oil in a large skillet over medium-high heat. Add pork chops and cook for about 4-5 minutes on each side or until they reach an internal temperature of 145°F (63°C).
3. Reduce heat to medium-low and pour the balsamic mixture over the pork chops. Simmer for 3-4 minutes, or until the sauce thickens and the pork chops are glazed.
4. Serve the pork chops with the glaze spooned over the top.

Nutritional Information:
300 calories, 25g protein, 15g carbohydrates, 12g fat, 0g fiber, 65mg cholesterol, 320mg sodium, 500mg potassium.

Balsamic Glazed Beef Skewers

Prep. time: 15 min | Cook time: 10 min | Serves: 4

Ingredients

- 1 pound lean beef sirloin, cut into 1-inch cubes
- 1/4 cup balsamic vinegar
- 2 tablespoons olive oil
- 2 cloves garlic, minced
- 1 tablespoon honey
- 1 teaspoon dried rosemary
- Salt and pepper to taste
- 1 red onion, cut into chunks
- 1 bell pepper, cut into chunks
- Wooden or metal skewers

Directions

1. Marinate the Beef: In a mixing bowl, whisk together balsamic vinegar, olive oil, minced garlic, honey, dried rosemary, salt, and pepper—toss to coat after adding the meat cubes. Put the lid on and let it marinade in the fridge for a minimum of two hours, but ideally overnight.
2. Grill Prep: Preheat your grill to medium-high. Soak wooden skewers in water for at least 30 minutes before use to prevent scorching.
3. Assemble Skewers: Thread the marinated beef, onion, and bell pepper alternately onto the skewers.
4. Grill Skewers: Grill the skewers for 5 minutes on each side or until the beef is cooked to your desired level.
5. Serve: Serve the skewers hot, drizzled with any remaining marinade that has been boiled for several minutes to reduce and thicken.

Nutritional Information:
Calories: 280, Protein: 26 g, Carbohydrates: 12 g, Fat: 14 g, Fiber: 1 g, Cholesterol: 70 mg, Sodium: 180 mg, Potassium: 450 mg

Lean Beef and Broccoli Stir-Fry

Prep. time: 15 min | Cook time: 10 min | Serves: 4

Ingredients

- 1 pound lean beef sirloin, thinly sliced against the grain
- 4 cups broccoli florets
- 2 tablespoons olive oil
- 2 cloves garlic, minced
- 1 tablespoon fresh ginger, minced
- 1/4 cup low-sodium soy sauce
- 1 tablespoon oyster sauce (optional)
- 1 tablespoon cornstarch
- 1/2 cup water
- 1 teaspoon sesame oil
- Salt and pepper to taste

Directions

1. Prepare Sauce: Combine the oyster sauce, cornstarch, soy sauce, and water in a small bowl and stir until well combined. Set aside.
2. Heat Oil: Heat the olive oil over medium-high heat in a large skillet or wok. Add the garlic and ginger and sauté until fragrant, about 1 minute.
3. Cook Beef: Add the sliced beef to the skillet and stir-fry it for three to four minutes or until the color becomes brown.
4. Add Broccoli: Add broccoli florets and the vegetables, stir-frying for 3–4 minutes until crisp-tender.
5. Incorporate Sauce: Drizzle the ready-made sauce over the beef and broccoli. Cook, constantly stirring, until the sauce becomes thick and evenly envelops the ingredients, approximately 2 minutes. Until the color starts to become brown. Season with salt and pepper and drizzle with sesame oil.
6. Serve: Remove from heat and serve immediately.

Nutritional Information:

Calories: 280, Protein: 26 g, Carbohydrates: 13 g, Fat: 14 g, Fiber: 3 g, Cholesterol: 55 mg, Sodium: 430 mg, Potassium: 700 mg.

Beef Tenderloin with Roasted Tomatoes

Prep. time: 10 min | Cook time: 25 min | Serves: 4

Ingredients

- 1 pound beef tenderloin
- 2 cups cherry tomatoes
- Three tablespoons olive oil
- 2 cloves garlic, minced
- 1 tablespoon fresh rosemary, chopped
- Salt and pepper to taste

Directions

1. Preheat Oven: Preheat your oven to 425°F (220°C).
2. Prepare the beef: Season the beef tenderloin with salt, pepper, and half of the chopped rosemary.
3. Heat one tablespoon of olive oil over medium-high heat in a roasting pan. Brown the tenderloin on all sides until it achieves a golden hue, approximately 3-4 minutes per side. Remove from the heat.
4. Prepare Tomatoes: In a bowl, toss the cherry tomatoes with olive oil, garlic, and rosemary. Spread the tomatoes around the beef in the roasting pan.
5. Bake: After warming the oven, place the pan inside and roast the beef for about 20 minutes or until the required doneness is achieved. Remove the meat and let it rest for 10 minutes before slicing. Serve with the roasted tomatoes.

Nutritional Information:

Calories: 320, Protein: 28 g, Carbohydrates: 6 g, Fat: 20 g, Fiber: 1 g, Cholesterol: 75 mg, Sodium: 65 mg, Potassium: 650 mg

Beef and Mushroom Stuffed Zucchini

Prep. time: 20 min | Cook time: 30 min | Serves: 4

Ingredients

- 4 medium zucchinis, halved lengthwise
- 1/2 pound lean ground beef
- 1 cup chopped mushrooms
- 1 onion, finely diced
- 2 cloves garlic, minced
- 1 cup low-sodium tomato sauce
- 1 teaspoon dried basil
- 1 teaspoon dried oregano
- 1/4 cup grated Parmesan cheese
- 1 tablespoon olive oil
- Salt and pepper to taste

Directions

1. Preheat Oven and Prepare Zucchini: Preheat your oven to 375°F (190°C). Scoop out the center of each zucchini half to create a boat, leaving about 1/4-inch of zucchini flesh along the sides.
2. Cook the Filling: Heat the olive oil in a skillet over medium heat. Add the ground beef, mushrooms, onion, and garlic. Cook until the meat is browned and the vegetables are softened about 8-10 minutes. Drain any excess fat.
3. Combine with Sauce: Stir in the tomato sauce, basil, and oregano. After five minutes of simmering, add salt and pepper to taste.
4. Stuff Zucchini: Spoon the beef and mushroom mixture into the hollowed-out zucchini boats and sprinkle grated Parmesan cheese.
5. Bake: Arrange the stuffed zucchini on a baking sheet and bake for 20 minutes in the oven until the zucchini is tender and the topping is bubbly and golden.

Nutritional Information:
Calories: 220, Protein: 18 g, Carbohydrates: 15 g, Fat: 10 g, Fiber: 3 g, Cholesterol: 40 mg, Sodium: 200 mg, Potassium: 900 mg

Italian Beef and Veggie Skillet

Prep. time: 15 min | Cook time: 20 min | Serves: 4

Ingredients

- 1 pound lean ground beef
- 1 medium zucchini, diced
- 1 red bell pepper, diced
- 1 onion, diced
- 2 cloves garlic, minced
- 1 cup chopped mushrooms
- 1 can (14.5 ounces) diced tomatoes, no salt added
- 1 teaspoon dried Italian seasoning
- 1/2 teaspoon salt
- 1/4 teaspoon black pepper
- 2 tablespoons olive oil
- Fresh basil, chopped (for garnish)

Directions

1. Heat the Skillet: Heat the olive oil over medium heat in a large skillet. Add the onion and garlic, and cook for approximately 3 minutes or until the onion turns translucent.
2. Cook the Beef: Fill the skillet with the ground beef. Break it up with a spatula and heat until browned, about five to seven minutes.
3. Add Vegetables: Stir in the zucchini, bell pepper, and mushrooms. Cook for about 5 minutes or until the vegetables are soft.
4. Add Tomatoes and Seasonings: Pour in the diced tomatoes (with their juice) and add Italian seasoning, salt, and pepper. Stir well to combine all ingredients—simmer for about five minutes to let the flavors blend.
5. Garnish and Serve: Remove from heat, garnish with fresh basil, and serve hot, possibly over whole wheat pasta or a side of crusty whole-grain bread.

Nutritional Information:
Calories: 280, Protein: 26 g, Carbohydrates: 15 g, Fat: 12 g, Fiber: 3 g, Cholesterol: 70 mg, Sodium: 320 mg, Potassium: 750 mg

Zesty Orange Beef Stir-Fry

Prep. time: 15 min | Cook time: 10 min | Serves: 4

Ingredients

- 1 pound lean beef sirloin, thinly sliced
- 2 tablespoons soy sauce (low sodium)
- Juice and zest of 1 large orange
- 1 tablespoon cornstarch
- 1 tablespoon olive oil
- 2 cloves garlic, minced
- 1 red bell pepper, sliced
- 1 cup snap peas
- 1 small onion, sliced
- 1 teaspoon grated ginger
- 1/2 teaspoon red pepper flakes (optional)
- Salt and pepper to taste
- Sesame seeds for garnish (optional)

Directions

1. Marinate Beef: In a bowl, combine the soy sauce, orange juice, orange zest, and cornstarch. Toss to coat after adding the sliced steak. Let it marinate for ten minutes.
2. Heating up the oil: Add the olive oil to a big skillet or wok and place over high heat. Stir-fry the garlic, ginger, and red pepper flakes for 30 seconds or until fragrant.
3. Cook Beef: Add the marinated beef to the skillet, spreading it into one layer. Let it sear without stirring for about 1 minute, then stir-fry for 2-3 minutes or until it browns.
4. Add Vegetables: Add the bell pepper, snap peas, and onion to the skillet. Stir-fry the vegetables for three to four minutes or until they are soft and the beef is done.
5. Season and Serve: To taste, add salt and pepper for seasoning. Garnish with sesame seeds if desired. Serve immediately, ideally over a bed of brown rice or quinoa.

Nutritional Information:
Calories: 250, Protein: 26 g, Carbohydrates: 14 g, Fat: 10 g, Fiber: 2 g, Cholesterol: 60 mg, Sodium: 350 mg, Potassium: 500 mg

Spicy Tomato Beef Tacos

Prep. time: 15 min | Cook time: 10 min | Serves: 4

Ingredients

- 1 pound lean ground beef
- 1 medium onion, diced
- 2 cloves garlic, minced
- 1 can of chopped tomatoes with green chiles, 14 ounces
- 1 teaspoon chili powder
- 1/2 teaspoon cumin
- 1/2 teaspoon paprika
- Salt and pepper to taste
- 8 small corn tortillas
- Fresh cilantro, chopped (for garnish)
- 1 lime, cut into wedges (for serving)
- Optional toppings: shredded lettuce, diced avocado, low-fat sour cream

Directions

1. In a large skillet over medium heat, cook the ground beef for five to seven minutes. Breaking it up with a spoon until it's browned.
2. Add Aromatics: Cook the onion and garlic in the skillet with the steak for about three minutes or until the onion is transparent.
3. Season: Stir in the diced tomatoes with green chilies, chili powder, cumin, paprika, salt, and pepper. Simmer for 5 minutes until the mixture is heated through and slightly thickened.
4. Prepare Tortillas: Warm the tortillas in a dry skillet or the microwave wrapped in a damp paper towel.
5. Assemble Tacos: Spoon the beef mixture into the warm tortillas. Top with fresh cilantro and optional toppings like lettuce, avocado, or a dollop of low-fat sour cream. Serve with lime wedges on the side.

Nutritional Information:
Calories: 290, Protein: 26 g, Carbohydrates: 22 g, Fat: 12 g, Fiber: 4 g, Cholesterol: 70 mg, Sodium: 300 mg, Potassium: 500 mg

Chapter 7. Vegan and Vegetarian

Chickpea and Spinach Curry

Prep. time: 10 min | Cook time: 20 min | Serves: 4

Ingredients

- 2 tablespoons olive oil
- 1 large onion, finely chopped
- 2 cloves garlic, minced
- 1 tablespoon grated fresh ginger
- 1 tablespoon curry powder
- 1 teaspoon ground cumin
- 1 can (15 oz) chickpeas, drained and rinsed
- 1 can (14 oz) diced tomatoes
- 4 cups fresh spinach leaves
- 1 can (14 oz) coconut milk
- Salt and pepper to taste
- Fresh cilantro, chopped (for garnish)

Directions

1. Sauté Aromatics: Heat the olive oil in a large skillet over medium heat. Add the onion, garlic, and ginger; simmer for about 5 minutes or until the onion becomes transparent.
2. Add Spices: Stir in the curry powder and cumin and cook until the spices are aromatic, about 1 minute more.
3. Combine Ingredients: Add the chickpeas, tomatoes, and coconut milk to the skillet. Bring to a simmer, lower the heat, and simmer for ten minutes to let the flavors meld.
4. Add spinach: Fold and cook until it collapses, approximately 3 minutes. Adjust the salt and pepper to taste.
5. Garnish and Serve: Serve the curry hot, garnished with chopped cilantro. It pairs wonderfully with basmati rice or naan bread.

Nutritional Information:
Calories: 350, Protein: 12 g, Carbohydrates: 30 g, Fat: 22 g, Fiber: 8 g, Cholesterol: 0 mg, Sodium: 300 mg, Potassium: 600 mg

Zucchini Noodle Pesto Pasta

Prep. time: 15 min | Cook time: 5 min | Serves: 4

Ingredients

- Four large zucchinis
- 1 cup fresh basil leaves
- 1/4 cup pine nuts
- 2 cloves garlic
- 1/4 cup grated Parmesan cheese
- 1/4 cup olive oil
- Salt and pepper to taste
- Cherry tomatoes for garnish (optional)

Directions

1. Make Zucchini Noodles: Use a spiralizer to turn the zucchini into noodles. Set aside in a large bowl.
2. Prepare Pesto Sauce: In a food processor, combine basil leaves, pine nuts, garlic, and Parmesan cheese. Pulse until coarsely chopped. Add olive oil while processing until the mixture becomes smooth and creamy—season with salt and pepper.
3. Combine Noodles and Pesto: Toss the zucchini noodles with the fresh pesto until evenly coated. You can serve the noodles raw or heat them gently in a skillet for 2-3 minutes if you prefer slightly warmed.
4. Serve: Divide the zucchini noodles among plates and garnish with cherry tomatoes if desired. Serve immediately.

Nutritional Information:
Calories: 250, Protein: 6 g, Carbohydrates: 8 g, Fat: 22 g, Fiber: 2 g, Cholesterol: 4 mg, Sodium: 180 mg, Potassium: 512 mg

Vegan Mushroom Stroganoff

Prep. time: 10 min | Cook time: 20 min | Serves: 4

Ingredients

- 1 pound mixed mushrooms (such as cremini, portobello, and shiitake), sliced
- 1 large onion, finely chopped
- 2 cloves garlic, minced
- 2 tablespoons olive oil
- 2 tablespoons all-purpose flour
- 2 cups vegetable broth
- 1 cup vegan sour cream
- 2 teaspoons Dijon mustard
- 1 teaspoon smoked paprika
- Salt and pepper to taste
- Fresh parsley, chopped (for garnish)
- Cooked whole wheat noodles or rice for serving

Directions

1. Sauté Vegetables: Warm the olive oil over medium heat in a big skillet. Add the onion and garlic, and cook for about 5 minutes or until the onion turns translucent.
2. Cook Mushrooms: Add the sliced mushrooms to the skillet and cook for about 10 minutes or until tender and browned. After dusting the mushrooms with flour, toss to coat.
3. Add liquids and season: Stir constantly, and pour the veggie broth to make a smooth sauce. After bringing to a simmer, cook for five minutes to thicken. Add the smoked paprika, vegan sour cream, and Dijon mustard—season with salt and pepper.
4. Simmer: Reduce heat and simmer the mixture for another 5 minutes, stirring occasionally.
5. Serve: Spoon the mushroom stroganoff over cooked whole wheat noodles or rice, garnish with chopped parsley, and serve immediately.

Nutritional Information:

Calories: 280, Protein: 8 g, Carbohydrates: 20 g, Fat: 20 g, Fiber: 3 g, Cholesterol: 0 mg, Sodium: 480 mg, Potassium: 600 mg

Cauliflower and Chickpea Tacos

Prep. time: 15 min | Cook time: 25 min | Serves: 4

Ingredients

- 1 head cauliflower, cut into small florets
- 1 can (15 oz) chickpeas, drained and rinsed
- 2 tablespoons olive oil
- 1 teaspoon chili powder
- 1 teaspoon paprika
- 1/2 teaspoon ground cumin
- Salt and pepper to taste
- 8 small corn tortillas
- 1 avocado, sliced
- 1/4 cup fresh cilantro, chopped
- Lime wedges for serving
- Optional toppings: diced tomatoes, shredded cabbage, salsa

Directions

1. Roast Cauliflower and Chickpeas: Preheat the oven to 400°F (200°C). Toss the cauliflower and chickpeas in a big bowl with olive oil, salt, pepper, cumin, paprika, chili powder, and oil until thoroughly covered. Place on an oven tray and bake for twenty to twenty-five minutes, stirring halfway through, until cauliflower is tender and chickpeas are slightly crispy.
2. Warm Tortillas: Wrap them in foil and place them in the oven during the last 5 minutes of roasting to warm them up.
3. Assemble Tacos: Fill each tortilla with a portion of the roasted cauliflower and chickpeas—add slices of avocado and sprinkle with fresh cilantro.
4. Add Toppings and Serve Top with additional toppings, such as diced tomatoes, shredded cabbage, or salsa. Serve with lime wedges on the side.

Nutritional Information:

Calories: 350, Protein: 12 g, Carbohydrates: 45 g, Fat: 15 g, Fiber: 12 g, Cholesterol: 0 mg, Sodium: 200 mg, Potassium: 800 mg

Lentil and Sweet Potato Shepherd's Pie

Prep. time: 20 min | Cook time: 40 min | Serves: 4

Ingredients

- 2 large sweet potatoes, peeled and cubed
- 1 cup dried green lentils, rinsed
- 1 onion, finely chopped
- 2 carrots, diced
- 2 cloves garlic, minced
- 1 cup frozen peas
- 1 tablespoon olive oil
- 2 tablespoons tomato paste
- 1 teaspoon dried thyme
- 1/2 teaspoon dried rosemary
- 2 cups vegetable broth
- Salt and pepper to taste
- 1/4 cup unsweetened almond milk
- 2 tablespoons vegan butter

Directions

1. Cook Sweet Potatoes: Place sweet potatoes in a large pot of salted water. Bring to a boil and simmer for 15 minutes or until soft. After draining, mash till smooth with vegan butter and almond milk. Season with salt and pepper.
2. Cook Lentils: Heat 3 cups of water in a separate pot to a boil. Add lentils and simmer until soft, roughly 20 minutes— Drain any remaining water.
3. Prepare the Vegetable Mixture: Heat olive oil in a large skillet over medium heat. Add onion, carrots, and garlic, cooking until softened, about 5 minutes. Stir in the cooked lentils, frozen peas, tomato paste, thyme, and rosemary. Pour vegetable broth and simmer until the mixture thickens, about 10 minutes— season with salt and pepper.
4. Assemble the Pie: Preheat the oven to 375°F (190°C). Spoon the lentil mixture into a baking dish. Distribute the pureed sweet potatoes uniformly across the Top.
5. Bake: Place the dish in the oven for 20 minutes or until the Top is slightly golden.
6. Serve: Let the shepherd's pie cool slightly before serving. This dish is ideal for a filling dinner.

Nutritional Information:
Calories: 290, Protein: 12 g, Carbohydrates: 54 g, Fat: 4 g, Fiber: 11 g, Cholesterol: 0 mg, Sodium: 300 mg, Potassium: 800 mg

Stuffed Bell Peppers with Quinoa

Prep. time: 10 min | Cook time: 20 min | Serves: 4

Ingredients

- 4 large bell peppers, tops cut off and seeds removed
- 1 cup quinoa, rinsed
- 2 cups vegetable broth
- 1 tablespoon olive oil
- 1 small onion, diced
- 2 cloves garlic, minced
- 1 zucchini, diced
- 1 cup mushrooms, chopped
- 1 can (15 oz) black beans, drained and rinsed
- 1 teaspoon cumin
- 1/2 teaspoon chili powder
- 1/4 teaspoon black pepper
- 1/2 cup fresh cilantro, chopped
- 1/2 cup shredded low-fat cheese (optional)

Directions

1.   Cook Quinoa: Bring the vegetable broth to a boil in a saucepan. Turn the heat down to a simmer, cover, and cook the quinoa for about 15 minutes or until all liquid has been absorbed.
2.   Assemble the vegetable mixture: Heat olive oil in a skillet over medium heat while the quinoa cooks. Sauté onion and garlic until translucent. Add zucchini and mushrooms, cooking until they are soft. Stir in black beans, cumin, chili powder, and black pepper.
3.   Combine Quinoa and Vegetables: Mix it into the skillet with the vegetables once the quinoa is cooked. Add chopped cilantro and adjust seasoning if necessary.
4.   Stuff Peppers: Spoon the quinoa and vegetable mixture into the hollowed-out bell peppers. If using, top with shredded cheese.
5.   Bake: The filled peppers should be put in a roasting tray. Cover with foil and bake at 350°F (175°C) for 20 minutes in a preheated oven. Remove the cover and bake for ten minutes if the cheese is not bubbling and browning.
6.   Serve: Allow the peppers to cool slightly before serving. They can be garnished with more fresh cilantro or a dollop of Greek yogurt.

Nutritional Information:
Calories: 280, Protein: 12 g, Carbohydrates: 45 g, Fat: 7 g, Fiber: 9 g, Cholesterol: 0 mg, Sodium: 300 mg, Potassium: 600 mg

Eggplant and Tofu Stir-Fry

Prep. time: 20 min | Cook time: 15 min | Serves: 4

Ingredients

- 1 large eggplant, cut into 1-inch cubes
- 14 ounces firm tofu, drained and cubed
- 2 tablespoons soy sauce (low sodium)
- 1 tablespoon sesame oil
- 2 cloves garlic, minced
- 1 tablespoon fresh ginger, minced
- 1 red bell pepper, sliced
- 1 green bell pepper, sliced
- 1 tablespoon hoisin sauce
- 1 teaspoon chili paste
- 2 teaspoons cornstarch dissolved in 2 tablespoons water
- Fresh basil leaves for garnish
- Rice or noodles for serving

Directions

1. Prepare Tofu and Eggplant: Press the tofu to remove excess water. In a bowl, toss the tofu with 1 tablespoon of soy sauce. In a separate bowl, sprinkle the eggplant with salt to draw out moisture; let sit for about 10 minutes, then rinse and dry.
2. Cook the Tofu: Heat half the sesame oil over medium-high heat in a large skillet or wok. Add the tofu and sauté until golden on all sides. Then, please remove it from the skillet and set it aside.
3. Stir-Fry Vegetables: Add the remaining sesame oil to the skillet. Sauté garlic and ginger for about 1 minute. Add the bell peppers and eggplant. Stir-fry until the vegetables begin to soften, approximately 5 minutes.
4. Combine Ingredients: Return the tofu to the skillet. Stir in hoisin sauce, chili paste, and the remaining soy sauce. Stir in the cornstarch mixture and simmer until the sauce thickens about 2 minutes.
5. Top with a few fresh basil leaves just before serving. Serve warm alongside rice or noodles.

Nutritional Information:
Calories: 210, Protein: 13 g, Carbohydrates: 18 g, Fat: 10 g, Fiber: 6 g, Cholesterol: 0 mg, Sodium: 320 mg, Potassium: 500 mg

Tomato Basil Zoodle Caprese

Ingredients

- 4 medium zucchinis, spiralized into noodles
- 2 cups cherry tomatoes, halved
- 1 cup fresh mozzarella balls, halved
- 1/4 cup fresh basil leaves, torn
- 3 tablespoons extra virgin olive oil
- 2 tablespoons balsamic vinegar
- Salt and black pepper to taste
- Optional: balsamic glaze for drizzling

Directions

1. Prepare Zoodles: Spiralize the zucchini into noodles and place them in a large mixing bowl.
2. Mix Ingredients: Add the halved cherry tomatoes, mozzarella balls, and fresh basil to the zoodles.
3. Dress the Salad: Drizzle with olive oil and balsamic vinegar. Gently toss everything together to combine—season with salt and pepper to taste.
4. Chill and Serve: Let the salad sit for approximately ten minutes to allow the flavors to combine. If desired, serve chilled with a drizzle of balsamic glaze.

Nutritional Information:
Calories: 250, Protein: 10 g, Carbohydrates: 12 g, Fat: 18 g, Fiber: 3 g, Cholesterol: 20 mg, Sodium: 200 mg, Potassium: 500 mg

Avocado and White Bean Salad Wraps

Ingredients

- 1 can (15 oz) white beans, drained and rinsed
- 1 ripe avocado, diced
- 1 small red onion, finely chopped
- 1 red bell pepper, diced
- 1/4 cup fresh cilantro, chopped
- Juice of 1 lime
- 2 tablespoons olive oil
- Salt and pepper to taste
- 4 large whole wheat tortillas
- Optional: lettuce leaves or baby spinach

Directions

1. Prepare the Salad: In a large bowl, combine white beans, diced avocado, chopped red onion, red bell pepper, and chopped cilantro.
2. Dress the Salad: Add lime juice and olive oil to the salad. Gently toss to coat all the ingredients, and flavor with salt and pepper to your liking.
3. Assemble the Wraps: Lay out the whole wheat tortillas and layer lettuce leaves or baby spinach on each, if using. Spoon an equal amount of the avocado and white bean salad onto each tortilla.
4. Wrap and Serve: Roll the tortillas tightly around the filling, tucking in the edges to form a wrap. Cut in half and serve immediately.

Nutritional Information:
Calories: 350, Protein: 12 g, Carbohydrates: 45 g, Fat: 15 g, Fiber: 12 g, Cholesterol: 0 mg, Sodium: 300 mg, Potassium: 800 mg

Creamy Coconut Vegetable Curry

Prep. time: 15 min | Cook time: 25 min | Serves: 4

Ingredients

- 1 tablespoon coconut oil
- 1 onion, chopped
- 2 cloves garlic, minced
- 1 tablespoon fresh ginger, grated
- 1 tablespoon curry powder
- 1 teaspoon turmeric
- 1/2 teaspoon cumin
- 1 small cauliflower, cut into florets
- 1 red bell pepper, diced
- 1 zucchini, diced
- 1 carrot, sliced
- 1 can (14 oz) chickpeas, drained and rinsed
- 1 can (14 oz) diced tomatoes
- 1 can (14 oz) coconut milk
- Salt and pepper to taste
- Fresh cilantro for garnish
- Cooked rice or naan bread for serving

Directions

1. Sauté Aromatics: Heat the coconut oil over medium heat in a large pot. Add the onion, garlic, ginger, and sauté until the onion is translucent, about 5 minutes.
2. Add Spices: Stir in curry powder, turmeric, and cumin. Cook for about 1 minute until fragrant.
3. Cook Vegetables: Add the cauliflower, bell pepper, zucchini, and carrot to the pot. Stir well to coat the vegetables in the spices.
4. Simmer with Liquids: Add the chickpeas, diced tomatoes, and coconut milk. Once the vegetables are soft, please bring them to a simmer and cook, covering them for 20 minutes.
5. Season and Serve: Season the curry with salt and pepper to taste. Serve hot cooked rice or with naan bread, garnished with fresh cilantro.

Nutritional Information:
Calories: 350, Protein: 9 g, Carbohydrates: 35 g, Fat: 22 g, Fiber: 8 g, Cholesterol: 0 mg, Sodium: 300 mg, Potassium: 800 mg

Spicy Peanut Tofu and Broccoli

Prep. time: 15 min | Cook time: 20 min | Serves: 4

Ingredients

- 14 ounces firm tofu, pressed and cubed
- 4 cups broccoli florets
- 2 tablespoons sesame oil
- 1/4 cup natural peanut butter
- 2 tablespoons soy sauce (low sodium)
- 1 tablespoon maple syrup or honey
- 1 tablespoon rice vinegar
- 1 teaspoon chili garlic sauce or sriracha
- 2 cloves garlic, minced
- 1-inch piece ginger, grated
- 1/2 cup water
    Optional: Crushed peanuts and green onions for garnish

Directions

1.   Cook the Tofu: Heat 1 tablespoon sesame oil over medium-high heat in a non-stick skillet. Add the tofu cubes and sauté until golden brown on all sides, approximately 10 minutes. Remove from skillet and set aside.
2.   Prepare Sauce: Within a little bowl, whisk together peanut butter, soy sauce, maple syrup, rice vinegar, chili garlic sauce, garlic, and ginger. Slowly stir in water until the mixture is smooth.
3.   Cook Broccoli: In the same skillet, add the remaining sesame oil and broccoli florets—Sauté for about 5 minutes or until the broccoli is bright green and tender-crisp.
4.   Combine and Simmer: Add the fried tofu back to the skillet along with the peanut sauce. Stir to coat the tofu and broccoli. Stirring regularly, simmer for five minutes, or until the sauce is thicker and everything is heated.
5.   Serve: Garnish with crushed peanuts and green onions if desired. Serve hot cooked rice or noodles.

Nutritional Information:
Calories: 300, Protein: 18 g, Carbohydrates: 20 g, Fat: 18 g, Fiber: 4 g, Cholesterol: 0 mg, Sodium: 300 mg, Potassium: 500 mg

Moroccan Vegetable Tagine

Prep. time: 20 min | Cook time: 40 min | Serves: 4

Ingredients

- 2 tablespoons olive oil
- 1 large onion, chopped
- 2 cloves garlic, minced
- 1 teaspoon ground cumin
- 1 teaspoon ground coriander
- 1 teaspoon ground cinnamon
- 1/2 teaspoon ground turmeric
- 1/2 teaspoon ground ginger
- 1 large carrot, sliced
- 1 sweet potato, cubed
- 1 zucchini, sliced
- 1 bell pepper, chopped
- 1 can (14 oz) diced tomatoes
- 1 can (15 oz) chickpeas, drained and rinsed
- 1/2 cup dried apricots, chopped
- 2 cups vegetable broth
- Salt and pepper to taste
- Fresh cilantro, chopped for garnish
- Cooked couscous or rice for serving

Directions

1. Sauté Aromatics: Heat olive oil in a large pot or tagine over medium heat.
2. Incorporate the onion and garlic and sauté until transparent. Stir in cumin, coriander, cinnamon, turmeric, and ginger, and cook for another minute until fragrant.
3. Add Vegetables: Add carrots, sweet potatoes, zucchini, and bell pepper to the pot. Toss will distribute the spices throughout the veggies.
4. Simmer with Liquids: Add the diced tomatoes with their juices, chickpeas, apricots, and vegetable broth. Bring to a boil, then lower the heat to a simmer and cover. Cook on low heat for about 30 minutes or until the vegetables are soft.
5. Season and Serve: Season the tagine with salt and pepper to taste. Serve hot cooked couscous or rice garnished with fresh cilantro.

Nutritional Information:
Calories: 280, Protein: 8 g, Carbohydrates: 45 g, Fat: 8 g, Fiber: 10 g, Cholesterol: 0 mg, Sodium: 300 mg, Potassium: 800 mg

Mediterranean Couscous Salad

Prep. time: 15 min | Cook time: 5 min | Serves: 4

Ingredients

- 1 cup whole wheat couscous
- 1 cup boiling water
- 1 cucumber, diced
- 1 red bell pepper, diced
- 1/2 red onion, finely chopped
- 1 cup cherry tomatoes, halved
- 1/4 cup kalamata olives, sliced
- 1/4 cup feta cheese, crumbled (optional)
- 1/4 cup fresh parsley, chopped
- 2 tablespoons olive oil
- Juice of 1 lemon
- Salt and pepper to taste

Directions

1. Prepare Couscous: Place the couscous in a large bowl. Cover with a lid or plastic wrap, pour boiling water over it, and let it sit for 5 minutes—fluff with a fork to separate grains.
2. Combine Ingredients: Add cucumber, red bell pepper, red onion, cherry tomatoes, olives, feta cheese (if using), and parsley to the fluffed couscous.
3. Dress Salad: Whisk olive oil and lemon juice in a small bowl. Pour over the salad and toss to combine—season with salt and pepper to taste.
4. Chill: Before serving, let the salad sit in the fridge for at least half an hour to bring out the best flavors.
5. Serve: Serve chilled or at room temperature.

Nutritional Information:
Calories: 280, Protein: 8 g, Carbohydrates: 40 g, Fat: 10 g, Fiber: 5 g, Cholesterol: 10 mg, Sodium: 200 mg, Potassium: 300 mg

Golden Turmeric Lentil Soup

Prep. time: 10 min | Cook time: 30 min | Serves: 4

Ingredients

- 1 cup red lentils, rinsed
- 1 tablespoon olive oil
- 1 large onion, chopped
- 2 garlic cloves, minced
- 1 tablespoon freshly grated ginger
- 1 teaspoon ground turmeric
- 1/2 teaspoon cumin
- 1/4 teaspoon black pepper
- 1 carrot, diced
- 1 celery stalk, diced
- 4 cups vegetable broth
- 1 can (14 oz) coconut milk
- Juice of 1 lemon
- Salt to taste
- Fresh cilantro, chopped for garnish

Directions

1. Sauté Aromatics: Heat the olive oil in a large pot over medium heat. Add the onion, garlic, and ginger, and sauté until translucent. Stir in the turmeric, cumin, and black pepper, cooking for another minute until fragrant.
2. Add Lentils and Vegetables: Add the rinsed lentils, diced carrot, and celery to the pot. Stir to combine and cook for a few minutes, letting the flavors meld.
3. Simmer: Add the vegetable broth and bring the mixture to a boil. Lower the heat and let it cook softly for about 20 minutes or until the lentils are soft.
4. Finish with Coconut Milk: Stir in the coconut milk and simmer for 10 minutes-incorporate the lemon juice and make any necessary salt seasoning adjustments.
5. Spoon the soup into individual bowls, top with finely chopped cilantro, and serve hot.

Nutritional Information:
Calories: 280, Protein: 10 g, Carbohydrates: 32 g, Fat: 12 g, Fiber: 9 g, Cholesterol: 0 mg, Sodium: 300 mg, Potassium: 600 mg

Ratatouille with Herbed Quinoa

Prep. time: 20 min | Cook time: 40 min | Serves: 4

Ingredients

- 1 cup quinoa, rinsed
- 2 cups vegetable broth
- 1 small eggplant, cubed
- 1 zucchini, sliced into half-moons
- 1 yellow squash, sliced into half-moons
- 1 bell pepper (any color), chopped
- 1 onion, chopped
- 3 cloves garlic, minced
- 1 can (14 oz) diced tomatoes
- 1 tablespoon fresh thyme, chopped
- 1 tablespoon fresh basil, chopped
- 2 tablespoons olive oil
- Salt and pepper to taste

Directions

1. Mix the quinoa and vegetable broth in a medium saucepan. After raising to a boil, lower the heat to a simmer, cover, and cook for approximately fifteen minutes, or until all liquid has been absorbed.
2. While the quinoa cooks, heat olive oil in a large skillet over medium heat. Add onion and garlic, sautéing until onion is translucent.
3. Add eggplant, zucchini, yellow squash, and bell pepper to the skillet. Cook for roughly 10 minutes, stirring occasionally, until vegetables are tender.
4. Stir in diced tomatoes and their juices, thyme, and basil. Simmer the ratatouille for another 10-15 minutes until thickened, then season with salt and pepper.
5. Serve the vegetable ratatouille over the cooked herbed quinoa.

Nutritional Information:
295 calories, 9g protein, 45g carbohydrates, 8g fat, 8g fiber, 0mg cholesterol, 320mg sodium, 770mg potassium.

Chapter 8. Sides and Vegetables

Garlic Roasted Green Beans

Prep. time: 10 min | Cook time: 20 min | Serves: 4

Ingredients

- 1 pound fresh green beans, trimmed
- 3 tablespoons olive oil
- 4 cloves garlic, minced
- Salt and pepper to taste
- Optional: lemon zest or almond slivers for garnish

Directions

1. Preheat Oven: Preheat your oven to 425°F (220°C).
2. Prepare Green Beans: Toss the green beans with olive oil and minced garlic in a big bowl, ensuring they are uniformly coated—season with salt and pepper.
3. Roast: Spread the green beans in a single layer on a baking sheet. Roast in the oven for about 20 minutes, or until the beans are tender and slightly browned, stirring halfway through cooking.
4. Garnish and Serve: For added flavor and crunch, sprinkle with lemon zest or almond slivers before serving.

Nutritional Information:
Calories: 120, Protein: 2 g, Carbohydrates: 10 g, Fat: 9 g, Fiber: 4 g, Cholesterol: 0 mg, Sodium: 10 mg, Potassium: 250 mg

Cumin-Spiced Carrot Fries

Prep. time: 10 min | Cook time: 25 min | Serves: 4

Ingredients

- 1 pound, peel, and thinly slice carrots
- 2 tablespoons olive oil
- 1 teaspoon ground cumin
- 1/2 teaspoon paprika
- Salt and pepper to taste
- Optional: Fresh parsley, chopped for garnish

Directions

1. Preheat Oven: Preheat your oven to 425°F (220°C).
2. Prepare Carrots: In a large bowl, toss the carrot sticks with olive oil, cumin, paprika, salt, and pepper until well coated.
3. Bake: Spread the carrots in a single layer on a baking sheet. Roast for about 25 minutes in a preheated oven, turning once halfway through, until crispy and golden.
4. Serve: Remove from the oven, garnish with chopped parsley if desired, and serve immediately.

Nutritional Information:
Calories: 120, Protein: 1 g, Carbohydrates: 14 g, Fat: 7 g, Fiber: 4 g, Cholesterol: 0 mg, Sodium: 170 mg, Potassium: 360 mg

Lemon-Garlic Asparagus Spears

Prep. time: 10 min | Cook time: 10 min | Serves: 4

Ingredients

- 1 pound fresh asparagus spears, trimmed
- 2 tablespoons olive oil
- 2 cloves garlic, minced
- Zest and juice of 1 lemon
- Salt and pepper to taste
- Optional garnish: grated Parmesan cheese or lemon slices

Directions

1. Preheat Oven: Preheat your oven to 400°F (200°C).
2. Prepare Asparagus: Arrange the spears in a single layer on a baking sheet.
3. Add Flavorings: In a small bowl, mix the olive oil, minced garlic, lemon zest, and lemon juice. Drizzle the asparagus with this mixture, toss to coat it evenly, and season with salt and pepper.
4. Roast: Place the asparagus in the oven and roast for 10 minutes until the spears are tender and slightly crisp.
5. Serve: Transfer the asparagus to a serving platter, sprinkle with Parmesan cheese if using, and garnish with additional lemon slices if desired.

Nutritional Information:
Calories: 90, Protein: 3 g, Carbohydrates: 6 g, Fat: 7 g, Fiber: 3 g, Cholesterol: 0 mg, Sodium: 2 mg, Potassium: 230 mg

Roasted Brussels Sprouts with Pomegranate

Prep. time: 10 min | Cook time: 20 min | Serves: 4

Ingredients

- 1 pound Brussels sprouts, trimmed and halved
- 2 tablespoons olive oil
- Salt and pepper to taste
- 1/2 cup pomegranate seeds
- 2 tablespoons balsamic vinegar
- Optional: 1 tablespoon of maple syrup or honey, optional for sweetness

Directions

1. Prepare the Oven: Pre-heat the oven to 400°F or 200°C.
2. Toss the sprouts with salt, pepper, and olive oil in a large bowl until well coated to prepare Brussels Sprouts.
3. Roast: Arrange the Brussels sprouts in a single layer on a baking sheet. Roast for 20 minutes in a preheated oven, stirring halfway through until they are crispy and tender.
4. Enhance Flavor: In the last few minutes of roasting, drizzle balsamic vinegar (and optional honey or maple syrup) over the Brussels sprouts for added flavor.
5. Serve with Pomegranate: Remove the Brussels sprouts from the oven, transfer to a serving dish, and sprinkle with pomegranate seeds before serving.

Nutritional Information:
Calories: 150, Protein: 4 g, Carbohydrates: 16 g, Fat: 8 g, Fiber: 5 g, Cholesterol: 0 mg, Sodium: 30 mg, Potassium: 450 mg

Balsamic Glazed Beetroot

Prep. time: 10 min | Cook time: 30 min | Serves: 4

Ingredients

- 4 medium beetroots, sliced into wedges after peeling
- 2 tablespoons olive oil
- Salt and pepper to taste
- 3 tablespoons balsamic vinegar
- 1 tablespoon of maple syrup or honey (optional for sweetness boost)
- Fresh thyme or rosemary (optional)

Directions

1. Preheat Oven: Preheat your oven to 400°F (200°C).
2. Prepare Beetroots: In a large bowl, toss the beetroot wedges with olive oil, salt, and pepper until well coated.
3. Roast Beetroots: Spread the beetroot on a baking sheet in a single layer. Preheat the oven and roast for about 25 minutes, flipping once halfway through or until they are soft and beginning to caramelize.
4. Glaze: In the last 5 minutes of cooking, drizzle the balsamic vinegar (and honey or maple syrup) over the beetroots. Return to the oven to finish roasting.
5. Serving meal: Remove the casserole from the oven, garnish with fresh thyme or rosemary, if desired, and serve warm.

Nutritional Information:
Calories: 140, Protein: 2 g, Carbohydrates: 18 g, Fat: 7 g, Fiber: 5 g, Cholesterol: 0 mg, Sodium: 80 mg, Potassium: 400 mg

Grilled Corn with Vegan Lime Butter

Prep. time: 10 min | Cook time: 10 min | Serves: 4

Ingredients

- 4 corn ears with their husks and silk removed
- 1/4 cup vegan butter, softened
- Zest and juice of 1 lime
- 1/2 teaspoon chili powder
- 1/4 teaspoon salt
- Fresh cilantro, chopped (optional for garnish)
- Lime wedges for serving

Directions

1. Grill Prepping: Set the temperature of your grill to medium-high.
2. Prepare Vegan Lime Butter: In a small bowl, mix the vegan butter, lime zest, lime juice, chili powder, and salt until well combined.
3. Grill Corn: Place corn directly on the grill grates. Grill the corn for about 10 minutes until it's cooked and has a light sear on all sides, flipping it occasionally.
4. Apply Vegan Lime Butter: Brush the corn off the grill with the vegan lime butter mixture.
5. Serve: Garnish with chopped cilantro and serve with extra lime wedges if preferred.

Nutritional Information:
Calories: 180, Protein: 3 g, Carbohydrates: 17 g, Fat: 12 g, Fiber: 2 g, Cholesterol: 0 mg, Sodium: 150 mg, Potassium: 250 mg

Creamy Cauliflower Mash

Prep. time: 10 min | Cook time: 15 min | Serves: 4

Ingredients

- 1 a big cauliflower head divided into florets
- 2 tablespoons olive oil
- 1/4 cup unsweetened almond milk
- 2 cloves garlic, minced
- Salt and pepper to taste
- Optional: Chives or parsley for garnish

Directions

1. Cook Cauliflower: Put the cauliflower florets in a big pot and add water to cover them. Bring to a boil, then simmer for ten minutes or until very soft. Drain well.
2. Mash: Return the drained cauliflower to the pot or place it in a large bowl. Add olive oil, almond milk, and minced garlic. It is using a potato masher or an immersion blender, puree the mixture until it's smooth and creamy.
3. Add salt and pepper to taste when seasoning. If necessary, add a little more almond milk to adjust the creaminess.
4. Serve: Transfer to a serving bowl, and if preferred, Top with chopped parsley or chives. Serve warm.

Nutritional Information:
Calories: 120, Protein: 3 g, Carbohydrates: 10 g, Fat: 8 g, Fiber: 4 g, Cholesterol: 0 mg, Sodium: 75 mg, Potassium: 470 mg

Citrusy Roasted Broccoli

Prep. time: 10 min | Cook time: 20 min | Serves: 4

Ingredients

- 1.5 pounds broccoli, cut into florets
- 2 tablespoons olive oil
- Zest and juice of 1 orange
- 2 cloves garlic, minced
- Salt and pepper to taste
- Optional: red pepper flakes for a bit of heat

Directions

1. Preheat Oven: Preheat your oven to 425°F (220°C).
2. Prepare Broccoli: In a large bowl, toss broccoli florets with olive oil, orange zest, orange juice, and minced garlic. Season with salt, pepper, and red pepper flakes.
3. Roast: Spread the broccoli in a single layer on a baking sheet—roast in the oven for 20 minutes or until the edges are crispy and slightly browned.
4. Serve: Remove from oven, give it a quick toss to refresh the flavors, and serve immediately.

Nutritional Information:
Calories: 130, Protein: 4 g, Carbohydrates: 12 g, Fat: 8 g, Fiber: 5 g, Cholesterol: 0 mg, Sodium: 30 mg, Potassium: 480 mg

Spiced Pumpkin Puree

Prep. time: 5 min | Cook time: 15 min | Serves: 4

Ingredients

- 2 cups pumpkin puree (fresh or canned)
- 2 tablespoons olive oil
- 1/2 teaspoon ground cinnamon
- 1/4 teaspoon ground nutmeg
- 1/4 teaspoon ground ginger
- 1/8 teaspoon ground cloves
- Salt to taste
- Optional: 1 tablespoon maple syrup or honey for sweetness

Directions

1. Heat Spices: In a medium saucepan, heat the olive oil over medium heat. Add cinnamon, nutmeg, ginger, and cloves. Stir for about 30 seconds until the spices release their aroma.
2. Combine with Pumpkin: Add the pumpkin puree to the saucepan. Stir well to combine with the spiced oil. Mix in maple syrup or honey for a touch of sweetness.
3. Simmer: Cook the mixture over medium-low heat for about 15 minutes, stirring periodically, until it is heated and the flavors melded together.
4. Season and Serve: Season with salt to taste. Serve warm as a side dish or as a base for other recipes.

Nutritional Information:
Calories: 140, Protein: 2 g, Carbohydrates: 18 g, Fat: 7 g, Fiber: 5 g, Cholesterol: 0 mg, Sodium: 75 mg, Potassium: 300 mg

Tangy Tomato and Cucumber Salad

Prep. time: 10 min | Cook time: 0 min | Serves: 4

Ingredients

- 3 large ripe tomatoes, chopped
- 1 large cucumber, peeled and diced
- 1/2 red onion, thinly sliced
- 1/4 cup fresh parsley, chopped
- 2 tablespoons olive oil
- 2 tablespoons red wine vinegar
- Salt and pepper to taste
- Optional: crumbled feta cheese or olives for garnish

Directions

1. Combine Vegetables: In a large bowl, combine the chopped tomatoes, diced cucumber, and sliced red onion.
2. Dress Salad: Add the chopped parsley, olive oil, and red wine vinegar to the bowl. Toss everything together to coat the vegetables evenly with the dressing—season with salt and pepper to taste.
3. Chill: Let the salad chill in the refrigerator for about 10 minutes before serving to allow the flavors to meld together.
4. Serve: Garnish with crumbled feta cheese or olives if desired. Serve chilled as a refreshing side dish.

Nutritional Information:
Calories: 120, Protein: 2 g, Carbohydrates: 10 g, Fat: 9 g, Fiber: 3 g, Cholesterol: 0 mg, Sodium: 10 mg, Potassium: 350 mg

Grilled Eggplant with Fresh Herbs

Prep. time: 10 min | Cook time: 10 min | Serves: 4

Ingredients

- 2 medium eggplants, sliced into 1/2-inch thick rounds
- 3 tablespoons olive oil
- Salt and pepper to taste
- 1/4 cup mixed fresh herbs (such as basil, parsley, and thyme), finely chopped
- 2 cloves garlic, minced
- Juice of 1 lemon

Directions

1. Preheat Grill: Preheat your grill to medium-high heat.
2. Prepare Eggplant: Brush both sides of the slices with olive oil and season with salt and pepper.
3. Grill Eggplant: Place the eggplant slices on the grill. Cook for 4-5 minutes on each side or until the eggplant is tender and grill marks appear.
4. Make Herb Mixture: Combine the chopped herbs, minced garlic, and lemon juice in a small bowl.
5. Serve: Once grilled, transfer the eggplant slices to a serving platter. Spoon the herb mixture over the warm eggplant and serve immediately.

Nutritional Information:
Calories: 160, Protein: 2 g, Carbohydrates: 15 g, Fat: 11 g, Fiber: 7 g, Cholesterol: 0 mg, Sodium: 10 mg, Potassium: 520 mg

Cauliflower Tabouli

Prep. time:15 min | Cook time: 0 min | Serves: 4

Ingredients

- 1 medium head of cauliflower, riced (about 4 cups)
- 1 cup fresh parsley, finely chopped
- 1/2 cup fresh mint, finely chopped
- 1/4 cup fresh lemon juice
- 1/4 cup olive oil
- 2 medium tomatoes, diced
- 1/2 cucumber, diced
- 2 green onions, thinly sliced
- Salt and pepper to taste

Directions

1. Prepare Cauliflower: Pulse cauliflower florets in a food processor until they resemble rice grains. Be careful not to overprocess them, as this can turn them mush.
2. Mix Ingredients: In a large bowl, combine the riced cauliflower, chopped parsley, mint, tomatoes, cucumber, and green onions.
3. Dress Salad: In a small bowl, whisk together lemon juice, olive oil, salt, and pepper: After pouring, thoroughly toss to coat the cauliflower mixture.
4. Chill and Marinate: To let the flavors meld, the tabouli should be allowed to sit in the refrigerator for at least 30 minutes before serving.
5. Serve: Adjust seasoning if necessary and serve chilled as a refreshing side dish.

Nutritional Information:
Calories: 180, Protein: 4 g, Carbohydrates: 15 g, Fat: 12 g, Fiber: 5 g, Cholesterol: 0 mg, Sodium: 30 mg, Potassium: 600 mg

Sweet Potato and Ginger Mash

Prep. time: 15 min | Cook time: 20 min | Serves: 4

Ingredients

- 4 large sweet potatoes, peeled and cubed
- 2 tablespoons olive oil
- 2 tablespoons fresh ginger, grated
- Salt and pepper to taste
- Optional: a pinch of cinnamon for extra flavor

Directions

1. Cook Sweet Potatoes: Put the sweet potato cubes in a big pot and add water to cover. Bring to a boil and cook until tender, about 15 minutes.
2. Drain and Mash: Drain the sweet potatoes well and return them to the pot. Mash the grated ginger and olive oil together until smooth. Add a dash of cinnamon and season with salt and pepper if preferred.
3. Adjust Texture: If the mash is too thick, add more olive oil or a splash of water to reach your desired consistency.
4. Serve: Serve the mash warm as a side dish, perfect alongside grilled or roasted meats, or as a comforting dish.

Nutritional Information:
Calories: 230, Protein: 3 g, Carbohydrates: 37 g, Fat: 7 g, Fiber: 6 g, Cholesterol: 0 mg, Sodium: 75 mg, Potassium: 670 mg

Minted Zucchini and Pea Salad

Prep. time:15 min | Cook time: 5 min | Serves: 4

Ingredients

- 2 medium zucchinis, thinly sliced or spiralized
- 1 cup fresh peas or thawed frozen peas
- 1/4 cup fresh mint leaves, chopped
- 2 tablespoons olive oil
- Juice of 1 lemon
- Salt and pepper to taste
- Optional: crumbled feta cheese or toasted pine nuts for garnish

Directions

1. Blanch Peas: If using fresh peas, blanch them in boiling water for 1-2 minutes until tender. Use frozen peas and ensure they are thawed completely.
2. Prepare Zucchini: Use a mandoline or a spiralizer to slice the zucchini into thin ribbons or noodles.
3. Mix Salad: In a large bowl, combine the zucchini, peas, and chopped mint. Toss with olive oil and lemon juice until everything is well coated. Season with salt and pepper.
4. Chill and Serve: Let the salad chill in the refrigerator for 10 minutes to allow flavors to meld. Serve chilled, garnished with feta cheese or toasted pine nuts if desired.

Nutritional Information:
Calories: 120, Protein: 4 g, Carbohydrates: 10 g, Fat: 8 g, Fiber: 3 g, Cholesterol: 0 mg, Sodium: 50 mg, Potassium: 350 mg

Chapter 9. Desserts Recipes

Apple Cinnamon Baked Oatmeal Cups

Prep. time: 10 min | Cook time: 25 min | Serves: 6

Ingredients

- 2 cups old-fashioned oats
- 1 teaspoon baking powder
- 1 1/2 teaspoons ground cinnamon
- 1/4 teaspoon salt
- 1 cup milk (any variety, dairy or non-dairy)
- 1/2 cup unsweetened applesauce
- 1 large apple, peeled and diced
- 1/4 cup honey or maple syrup
- 1 large egg
- 1 teaspoon vanilla extract
- Optional: nuts or raisins for added texture

Directions

1. Preheat Oven and Ready Pan: Turn the oven's temperature to 375°F (190°C). Grase or use paper liners to line a muffin pan.
2. Combine the dry ingredients: Mix the oats, cinnamon, baking powder, and salt in a big bowl.
3. Mix Wet Ingredients: In a separate bowl, beat milk, applesauce, honey, egg, and vanilla essence.
4. Blend Concoctions: Mix the dry ingredients with the wet ones until well blended. Fold in the diced apple, and if using, nuts or raisins.
5. Bake: Spoon the mixture into the prepared muffin tin, filling each cup until almost complete. Once the toothpick placed into the center of a muffin comes out clean, bake for 25 minutes or until the tops are brown.
6. Cool and Serve: After allowing the oatmeal cups to cool in the pan for ten minutes, move them to a wire rack to finish cooling.

Nutritional Information:
Calories: 220, Protein: 6 g, Carbohydrates: 38 g, Fat: 5 g, Fiber: 4 g, Cholesterol: 31 mg, Sodium: 125 mg, Potassium: 200 mg

Chia Seed Pudding with Mixed Berries

Prep. time:10 min | Cook time: 5 min (plus at least 4 hours for chilling) | Serves: 4

Ingredients

- 1/4 cup chia seeds
- 1 cup unsweetened almond milk (or any other milk of your choice)
- 1 tablespoon honey or maple syrup
- 1/2 teaspoon vanilla extract
- 1 cup of mixed berries, including raspberries, strawberries, and blueberries, fresh or frozen
- Optional toppings: additional berries, a sprinkle of granola, or coconut flakes

Directions

1. Mix the Pudding: In a bowl, combine the chia seeds, almond milk, honey (or maple syrup), and vanilla extract. Stir well to mix.
2. Chill: Cover the bowl and refrigerate for at least 4 hours, or overnight, until the chia seeds have absorbed the liquid and the mixture has a thick, pudding-like consistency.
3. Prepare Berries: If using frozen berries, thaw them in the refrigerator while the pudding is chilling. If fresh berries are used, wash them and prepare them before serving.
4. Assemble and Serve: Stir the pudding again and spoon it into serving dishes. Top with mixed berries and any additional toppings of your choice.

Nutritional Information:
Calories: 150, Protein: 4 g, Carbohydrates: 21 g, Fat: 6 g, Fiber: 8 g, Cholesterol: 0 mg, Sodium: 60 mg, Potassium: 200 mg

Avocado Chocolate Mousse

Prep. time: 15 min | Cook time: 0 min | Serves: 4

Ingredients

- 2 ripe avocados, peeled and pitted
- 1/4 cup unsweetened cocoa powder
- 1/4 cup honey or maple syrup (adjust to taste)
- 1/4 cup unsweetened almond milk (or any milk of your choice)
- 1 teaspoon vanilla extract
- Pinch of salt

Directions

1. Mix well. I ingredients: Put the avocados, cocoa powder, almond milk, vanilla extract, honey (or maple syrup), and a dash of salt in a blender or food processor. P process the mixture until it becomes creamy and smooth.
2. Adjust Flavor: Taste and adjust the sweetness if necessary. If the mousse is too thick, add more almond milk until it reaches the right consistency.
3. Chill: Transfer the mousse to a bowl and refrigerate for at least 30 minutes to allow the flavors to meld together and the mousse to thicken slightly.
4. Serve: Spoon the mousse into individual serving dishes and, if desired, garnish with fresh berries, shaved chocolate, or a sprinkle of powdered sugar.

Nutritional Information:
Calories: 250, Protein: 4 g, Carbohydrates: 30 g, Fat: 15 g, Fiber: 7 g, Cholesterol: 0 mg, Sodium: 30 mg, Potassium: 600 mg

Banana Almond Smoothie Bowl

Prep. time:10 min | Cook time: 0 min | Serves: 2

Ingredients

- 2 ripe bananas, frozen
- 1/4 cup almond butter
- 1/2 cup unsweetened almond milk
- 1 tablespoon chia seeds
- 1/2 teaspoon vanilla extract
- Toppings: Sliced almonds, fresh banana slices, chia seeds, shredded coconut, or fresh berries

Directions

1. Blend Smoothie: In a blender, combine the frozen bananas, almond butter, almond milk, chia seeds, and vanilla extract. Blend until smooth and creamy. Add more almond milk to modify the consistency if needed.
2. Prepare Bowls: Pour the smoothie mixture into two bowls.
3. Add Toppings: Garnish each bowl with sliced almonds, banana slices, extra chia seeds, shredded coconut, and berries of your choice.
4. Serve Immediately: Enjoy this smoothie bowl fresh for the best taste and texture.

Nutritional Information:
Calories: 340, Protein: 8 g, Carbohydrates: 40 g, Fat: 18 g, Fiber: 7 g, Cholesterol: 0 mg, Sodium: 80 mg, Potassium: 600 mg

Coconut Yogurt Parfait with Fresh Fruit

Prep. time: 10 min | Cook time: 0 min | Serves: 4

Ingredients

- 2 cups coconut yogurt (unsweetened)
- 1 cup granola (low-sugar or homemade)
- 1 cup fresh berries (such as strawberries, blueberries, and raspberries)
- 1 banana, sliced
- 1/2 cup chopped mixed nuts (like almonds and walnuts)
- Optional: honey or maple syrup for drizzling

Directions

1. Layer the Parfait: In each serving glass or bowl, start by layering a spoonful of coconut yogurt.
2. Add Granola and Fruit: Follow the yogurt with a layer of granola, then a layer of mixed fresh berries and banana slices.
3. Repeat Layers: Repeat the layering process until the glasses are filled to the top, ending with a layer of coconut yogurt.
4. Garnish: Top each parfait with chopped nuts and a drizzle of honey or maple syrup if desired.
5. Serve Immediately: You can enjoy these parfaits immediately or refrigerate them for an hour before serving to let the flavors meld together slightly.

Nutritional Information:
Calories: 350, Protein: 10 g, Carbohydrates: 40 g, Fat: 18 g, Fiber: 5 g, Cholesterol: 0 mg, Sodium: 60 mg, Potassium: 300 mg

Peach and Raspberry Sorbet

Prep. time:10 min | Cook time: 5 min (plus freezing time) | Serves: 4

Ingredients

- 2 cups fresh peaches, peeled and diced
- 1 cup fresh raspberries
- 1/2 cup water
- 1/2 cup sugar (or honey for a natural alternative)
- Juice of 1 lemon

Directions

1. Prepare the Fruit: In a blender, combine the peaches, raspberries, water, sugar, and lemon juice. Blend until the mixture is completely smooth.
2. Chill the Mixture: Pour the fruit mixture into a shallow container and chill in the refrigerator for at least 1 hour to ensure it is thoroughly cold.
3. Freeze: Pour the cold mixture into an ice cream maker and process until it reaches a sorbet consistency, following the manufacturer's directions. If you do not have an ice cream machine, pour the cold mixture into a shallow dish and freeze, stirring every 30 minutes to break up ice crystals, until frozen (approximately 2-3 hours).
4. Serve: To serve, take out the frozen sorbet and place it into glasses or bowls. Feel free to serve straight after or keep in an airtight container in the freezer for later use.

Nutritional Information:
Calories: 160, Protein: 1 g, Carbohydrates: 40 g, Fat: 0.5 g, Fiber: 3 g, Cholesterol: 0 mg, Sodium: 2 mg, Potassium: 210 mg

Dark Chocolate-Dipped Strawberries

Prep. time: 15 min | Cook time: 5 min (plus chilling time) | Serves: 4

Ingredients

- 16 large fresh strawberries, washed and patted dry
- 6 ounces dark chocolate (70% cocoa or higher), chopped
- Optional toppings: chopped nuts, coconut flakes, or white chocolate drizzle

Directions

1. Prepare Strawberries: The chocolate will seize if the strawberries aren't completely dried.
2. Melt Chocolate: Place the chopped dark chocolate in a heatproof bowl. Microwave, stirring between each 30-second burst, until well melted and smooth. Alternatively, use a double boiler on the stove to melt the chocolate.
3. Dip Strawberries: Hold each strawberry by the stem and dip it into the melted chocolate, swirling it to cover most of the fruit—let the excess chocolate drip off.
4. Add Toppings: Before the chocolate sets, immediately sprinkle with chopped nuts or coconut flakes. For a fancier finish, drizzle with melted white chocolate.
5. Chill: Place the chocolate-dipped strawberries on a baking sheet lined with parchment paper. Hill for about half an hour or until the chocolate solidifies.
6. Serve: Enjoy these strawberries as a decadent dessert or a special treat.

Nutritional Information:
Calories: 220, Protein: 3 g, Carbohydrates: 20 g, Fat: 14 g, Fiber: 4 g, Cholesterol: 0 mg, Sodium: 20 mg, Potassium: 250 mg

Vanilla Chia Pudding with Kiwi

Prep. time:10 min | Cook time: 0 min (plus at least 4 hours for chilling) | Serves: 4

Ingredients

- 1/4 cup chia seeds
- 1 cup unsweetened almond milk (or any other milk of your choice)
- 1 teaspoon vanilla extract
- 2 tablespoons honey or maple syrup
- 2 ripe kiwis, peeled and sliced

Directions

1. Mix the Pudding: In a bowl, combine the chia seeds, almond milk, vanilla extract, and honey or maple syrup. Whisk until well mixed.
2. Chill: Once the mixture has thickened into the consistency of pudding and the chia seeds have absorbed the liquid, cover the bowl with plastic wrap and refrigerate for at least 4 hours or overnight.
3. Prepare Kiwi: Just before serving, peel and slice the kiwis.
4. Assemble and Serve: Stir the pudding once more to check the consistency. Spoon into serving dishes, and top each with sliced kiwi.

Nutritional Information:
Calories: 130, Protein: 3 g, Carbohydrates: 19 g, Fat: 5 g, Fiber: 5 g, Cholesterol: 0 mg, Sodium: 40 mg, Potassium: 230 mg

No-Bake Peanut Butter Oat Bars

Prep. time: 15 min | Cook time: 20 min | Serves: 4

Ingredients

- 1 cup natural peanut butter (smooth or crunchy)
- 1/4 cup honey or maple syrup
- 1/2 cup coconut oil
- 2 cups rolled oats
- 1/2 cup dried cranberries or raisins
- 1/4 cup ground flaxseed (optional for added fiber)
- 1 teaspoon vanilla extract

Directions

1. Prepare the Mixture: In a medium saucepan, combine peanut butt r, honey, and coconut oil. Cook over low heat until the roughly blended and smooth. Take off the heat and mix in the vanilla essence.
2. Mix Dry Ingredients: Place rolled oats, dried cranberries, and ground flaxseed in a large bowl.
3. Mix All Ingredients: Pour the warm peanut butter mixture over the oat mixture and stir until everything is well coated and combined.
4. Press into Pan: Line an 8x8-inch baking pan with parchment paper. Transfer the mixture to the pan and press firmly into an even layer.
5. Chill: Refrigerate for at least 2 hours or until firm. Once set, cut into bars.
6. Serve or Store: Serve immediately or keep chilled for up to a week in an airtight container.

Nutritional Information:

Calories: 340, Protein: 8 g, Carbohydrates: 38 g, Fat: 20 g, Fiber: 5 g, Cholesterol: 0 mg, Sodium: 75 mg, Potassium: 240 mg

Carrot and Walnut Energy Bites

Prep. time:20 min | Cook time: 0 min | Serves: 6

Ingredients

- 1 cup finely grated carrots
- 1 cup rolled oats
- 1/2 cup finely chopped walnuts
- 1/4 cup ground flaxseed
- 1/2 cup peanut butter or almond butter
- 1/4 cup honey or maple syrup
- 1 teaspoon cinnamon
- 1/2 teaspoon nutmeg
- Optional: 1/4 cup shredded coconut for coating

Directions

1. Mix Ingredients: In a large bowl, combine the grated carrots, rolled oats, chopped walnuts, ground flaxseed, ci namon, and nutmeg. Stir to mix well.
2. Bind the Mixture: Combine the dry ingredients with the peanut butter and honey (or maple syrup). Mix thoroughly until everything is well combined and the mixture sticks together.
3. Form Bites: Using your hands, roll the mixture into small balls, about the size of a tablespoon each.
4. Coat Optionally: If using shredded coconut, roll each ball in coconut to coat the outside.
5. Chill: Transfer the energy bites to a parchment-lined baking sheet. To set, refrigerate for at least one hour.

Nutritional Information:

Calories: 250, Protein: 7 g, Carbohydrates: 28 g, Fat: 14 g, Fiber: 5 g, Cholesterol: 0 mg, Sodium: 75 mg, Potassium: 350 mg

Vegan Blueberry Muffins

Prep. time:15 min | Cook time: 25 min | Serves: 6

Ingredients

- 1 1/2 cups all-purpose flour (or use whole wheat flour for more fiber)
- 1/2 cup sugar (or substitute with coconut sugar)
- 1/2 teaspoon salt
- 2 teaspoons baking powder
- 1/3 cup vegetable oil
- 1 cup unsweetened almond milk
- 1 teaspoon vanilla extract
- 1 cup fresh or frozen blueberries

Directions

1. Preheat Oven and Prepare Pan: Preheat the oven to 375°F (190°C). Line a muffin pan with paper liners or lightly oil the cups.
2. Blend the dry ingredients: In a large bowl, mix the flour, sugar, salt, and baking powder together. Mix well to distribute the baking powder evenly.
3. Add Wet Ingredients: In a separate basin, mix the almond milk, vanilla essence, and vegetable oil. Mix until just mixed, and pour the wet components into the dry ingredients. Be careful not to blend too much.
4. Fold in Blueberries: Gently fold the blueberries into the batter, taking care not to crush them if they are fresh.
5. Bake: Spoon the batter into the prepared muffin tin, filling each cup about three-quarters full. After 25 minutes of baking, a toothpick put into the center of a muffin should come out clean.
6. Cool and Serve: After letting the muffins cool in the pan for five minutes, move them to a wire rack to finish cooling.

Nutritional Information:

Calories: 280, Protein: 4 g, Carbohydrates: 42 g, Fat: 10 g, Fiber: 2 g, Cholesterol: 0 mg, Sodium: 300 mg, Potassium: 120 mg

Coconut Rice Pudding with Mango

Prep. time:5 min | Cook time: 25 min | Serves: 4

Ingredients

- 1 cup Arborio rice or other short-grain rice
- 1 can (14 oz) coconut milk
- 2 cups water
- 1/4 cup sugar
- 1 teaspoon vanilla extract
- 1 ripe mango, peeled and diced
- Optional: Toasted coconut flakes for garnish

Directions

1. Cook the Rice: In a medium saucepan, mix rice, coconut milk, water, and sugar. Reduce heat after ringing to a boil. Cover and boil after 20 to 25 minutes or when the rice is tender and the stew has thickened, stirring occasionally.
2. Add Flavor: Stir in the vanilla extract after the rice is cooked. Leave it for a few minutes after turning off the heat to make it even thicker.
3. Prepare Mango: While the rice pudding cools, peel and dice the mango.
4. Serve: Spoon rice pudding into serving bowls. Top each with a generous portion of diced mango and sprinkle with toasted coconut flakes, if desired. This pudding can be enjoyed warm or chilled. If you prefer it chilled, refrigerate for at least 1 hour before serving.

Nutritional Information:

Calories: 310, Protein: 4 g, Carbohydrates: 50 g, Fat: 12 g, Fiber: 2 g, Cholesterol: 0 mg, Sodium: 30 mg, Potassium: 200 mg

Fig and Honey Yogurt Parfait

Prep. time: 10 min | Cook time: 0 min | Serves: 4

Ingredients

- 2 cups Greek yogurt, unsweetened
- 4 tablespoons honey, divided
- 1 teaspoon vanilla extract
- 8 fresh figs, washed and quartered
- 1/2 cup granola
- Optional: a sprinkle of cinnamon or chopped nuts for extra flavor and crunch

Directions

1. Prepare Yogurt Mixture: Mix the Greek yogurt with 2 tablespoons of honey and vanilla extract until smooth.
2. Assemble the Parfaits: In serving bowls or glasses, layer the yogurt mixture, granola, and quartered figs. Start with a layer of yogurt, then a spoonful of granola, and top with figs.
3. Drizzle Honey: Drizzle the remaining honey over each parfait layer, especially the top fig layer.
4. Garnish and Serve: Optionally, sprinkle each parfait with cinnamon or chopped nuts for added flavor and texture. Serve immediately for the best taste, or chill in the refrigerator for up to an hour before serving.

Nutritional Information:

Calories: 280, Protein: 12 g, Carbohydrates: 50 g, Fat: 5 g, Fiber: 3 g, Cholesterol: 10 mg, Sodium: 65 mg, Potassium: 240 mg

Carrot Cake with Yogurt Frosting

Prep. time: 20 min | Cook time: 30 min | Serves: 6

Ingredients

- For the Cake:
- 1 1/2 cups whole wheat flour
- 1 teaspoon baking powder
- 1/2 teaspoon baking soda
- 1 teaspoon ground cinnamon
- 1/2 teaspoon nutmeg
- 1/4 teaspoon salt
- 1/2 cup unsweetened applesauce
- 1/4 cup olive oil
- 1/2 cup honey or maple syrup
- 2 large eggs
- 1 teaspoon vanilla extract
- 2 cups grated carrots
- 1/2 cup chopped walnuts (optional)
- For the Yogurt Frosting:
- 1 cup Greek yogurt
- 2 tablespoons honey or maple syrup
- 1/2 teaspoon vanilla extract

Directions

1. Prepare Cake Batter:
   o Preheat the oven to 350°F (175°C). Utter and dust a 9-inch circular cake pan.
   o Mix the flour, baking powder, baking soda, nutmeg, cinnamon, and salt in a big bowl.
   o Whisk together the applesauce, eggs, honey, olive oil, and vanilla in a separate bowl.
   o Combine the dry and wet components by gently mixing them. If desired, fold in the grated carrots and walnuts.
2. Bake:
   o Spoon the batter into the prepared cake pan. Ake for 25–30 minutes or until a toothpick inserted into the center comes clean.
   o After removing it from the oven, let it cool in the pan for 10 minutes before transferring it to a wire rack to complete the cooling process.
3. To make the frosting, combine the Greek yogurt, honey, and vanilla extract in a bowl and mix until smooth.
4. Frost Cake: Once the cake is completely cool, spread the yogurt frosting evenly.
5. Serve or Store: If serving later, place in the refrigerator or serve immediately. When cooled, the frosting will become slightly firmer.

Nutritional Information:

Calories: 320, Protein: 8 g, Carbohydrates: 46 g, Fat: 12 g, Fiber: 4 g, Cholesterol: 62 mg, Sodium: 220 mg, Potassium: 230 mg

Baked Pear with Honey and Walnuts

Prep. time: 10 min | Cook time: 25 min | Serves: 4

Ingredients

- 4 ripe pears, halved and cored
- 4 teaspoons honey
- 1/2 cup walnuts, chopped
- 1/2 teaspoon ground cinnamon
- Optional: Greek yogurt or low-fat ice cream for serving

Directions

1. Preheat Oven: Preheat your oven to 350°F (175°C).
2. Prepare Pears: Arrange and cut the pear halves in a baking dish.
3. Add Toppings: Drizzle each pear half with honey, then sprinkle with chopped walnuts and a dusting of cinnamon.
4. Bake: Place the baking dish in the oven and bake for 25 minutes, or until the pears are tender and the nuts are toasted.
5. Serve: Serve the baked pears warm, optionally with a dollop of Greek yogurt or a scoop of low-fat ice cream on the side.

Nutritional Information:
Calories: 210, Protein: 3 g, Carbohydrates: 30 g, Fat: 10 g, Fiber: 6 g, Cholesterol: 0 mg, Sodium: 2 mg, Potassium: 210 mg

Chapter 10. Sauces and Condiments

Golden Turmeric Tahini Dressing

Prep. time:5 min | Cook time: 0 min | Serves: 4

Ingredients

- 1/3 cup tahini
- 1/4 cup lemon juice
- 2 tablespoons olive oil
- 1 tablespoon apple cider vinegar
- 1 teaspoon turmeric powder
- 1 clove garlic, minced
- 1/2 teaspoon ground cumin
- Salt and pepper to taste
- 2-4 teaspoons of water, depending on the required consistency

Directions

1. Combine Ingredients: In a bowl, whisk together tahini, lemon juice, olive oil, apple cider vinegar, turmeric, minced garlic, and cumin until smooth.
2. Adjust Consistency: Gradually add water, one tablespoon at a time, until the dressing reaches your preferred consistency. It should be creamy but pourable.
3. Season: Use salt and pepper to taste and adjust the seasoning.
4. Serve or Store: Use immediately over salads, roasted vegetables, or as a dip. Alternatively, store in an airtight container in the refrigerator for up to one week. Shake or stir well before using if separated.

Nutritional Information:
Calories: 180, Protein: 3 g, Carbohydrates: 8 g, Fat: 16 g, Fiber: 2 g, Cholesterol: 0 mg, Sodium: 20 mg, Potassium: 90 mg

Spicy Mango Chutney

Prep. time: 10 min | Cook time: 30 min | Serves: 4

Ingredients

- 2 large ripe mangoes, peeled and diced
- 1 red onion, finely chopped
- 1/2 cup apple cider vinegar
- 1/2 cup brown sugar
- 1/4 cup raisins
- 2 garlic cloves, minced
- 1 tablespoon fresh ginger, grated
- 1 teaspoon ground cinnamon
- 1/2 teaspoon ground cloves
- 1/2 teaspoon red chili flakes
- Salt to taste

Directions

1. Combine Ingredients: In a medium saucepan, combine all ingredients. Stir well to mix.
2. Simmer: Bring the mixture to a boil over medium heat. Reduce the heat and simmer for about 30 minutes, stirring now and again. The chutney should thicken as it cooks.
3. Cool: After taking the saucepan off the stove, allow the chutney to cool. As it cools, it will get thicker.
4. Store: Transfer the chutney to a clean jar and store it in the refrigerator. Allow it to marinate for at least a day before use to develop the flavors fully.

Nutritional Information:
Calories: 200, Protein: 1 g, Carbohydrates: 50 g, Fat: 0.5 g, Fiber: 2 g, Cholesterol: 0 mg, Sodium: 5 mg, Potassium: 200 mg

Avocado Cilantro Lime Sauce

Prep. time:10 min | Cook time: 0 min | Serves: 4

Ingredients

- 1 ripe avocado, peeled and pitted
- 1/2 cup fresh cilantro, roughly chopped
- Juice of 2 limes
- 1 clove garlic, minced
- 1/4 cup plain Greek yogurt (use non-fat for lower cholesterol)
- 2 tablespoons olive oil
- Salt and pepper to taste
- Water, as needed for thinning

Directions

1. Blend Ingredients: In a blender or food processor, combine the avocado, cilantro, lime juice, garlic, Greek yogurt, and olive oil. Blend until smooth.
2. Adjust Consistency: If the sauce is too thick, add water, one tablespoon at a time, until you reach the desired consistency.
3. Season: Use salt and pepper to taste and adjust the seasoning.
4. Serve or Store: Use immediately as a dressing, dip, or sauce, or store in an airtight container in the refrigerator for up to 3 days.

Nutritional Information:
Calories: 150, Protein: 2 g, Carbohydrates: 8 g, Fat: 13 g, Fiber: 4 g, Cholesterol: 0 mg, Sodium: 5 mg, Potassium: 400 mg

Tomato Basil Marinara

Prep. time: 10 min | Cook time: 30 min | Serves: 4

Ingredients

- 1 tablespoon olive oil
- 1 small onion, finely chopped
- 2 garlic cloves, minced
- 1 can (28 ounces) crushed tomatoes
- 1/4 cup fresh basil leaves, chopped
- 1 teaspoon dried oregano
- Salt and pepper to taste
- Optional: 1/2 teaspoon red pepper flakes for a bit of heat

Directions

1. Sauté Onions and Garlic: Heat the olive oil over medium heat in a large saucepan. Add the onion and garlic, sauté until the onion is translucent, for about 5 minutes.
2. Add Tomatoes and Seasonings: Stir in the crushed tomatoes, basil, oregano, and optional red pepper flakes. Bring to a simmer.
3. Simmer: Reduce heat to low and let the sauce simmer gently for about 25 minutes, stirring occasionally. The sauce should thicken slightly.
4. Season: Use salt and pepper to taste and adjust the seasoning. Remove from heat.
5. Serve or Store: Use immediately over pasta as a base for pizza, or cool and store in an airtight container in the refrigerator for up to one week or freeze for more extended storage.

Nutritional Information:
Calories: 90, Protein: 2 g, Carbohydrates: 13 g, Fat: 4 g, Fiber: 3 g, Cholesterol: 0 mg, Sodium: 300 mg, Potassium: 450 mg

Zesty Orange-Ginger Dressing

Prep. time:10 min | Cook time: 0 min | Serves: 4

Ingredients

- Juice of 2 large oranges (about 1/2 cup)
- 1 tablespoon grated fresh ginger
- 1 clove garlic, minced
- 2 tablespoons apple cider vinegar
- 1/4 cup olive oil
- 1 teaspoon honey (optional for sweetness)
- Salt and pepper to taste

Directions

1. Blend Ingredients: In a blender or using a whisk, combine orange juice, grated ginger, minced garlic, apple cider vinegar, olive oil, and honey, if using. Blend or whisk until thoroughly combined.
2. Season: Add salt and pepper to taste. If needed, adjust the sweetness or acidity by adding more honey or vinegar.
3. Chill: For the best flavor, chill the dressing in the refrigerator for at least 30 minutes before serving. This allows the flavors to meld together.
4. Serve or Store: Drizzle over your favorite salads or use it as a marinade for chicken or fish. Any leftover dressing can be stored in an airtight container in the refrigerator for up to one week.

Nutritional Information:
Calories: 140, Protein: 0 g, Carbohydrates: 6 g, Fat: 12 g, Fiber: 0 g, Cholesterol: 0 mg, Sodium: 5 mg, Potassium: 50 mg

Pomegranate Mint Relish

Prep. time: 15 min | Cook time: 0 min | Serves: 4

Ingredients

- 1 cup fresh pomegranate seeds
- 1/4 cup finely chopped fresh mint
- 1 small red onion, finely diced
- Juice of 1 lime
- 1 teaspoon honey (optional; adjust to taste)
- Salt and pepper to taste

Directions

1. Combine Ingredients: In a medium bowl, mix the pomegranate seeds, chopped min, red onion, and lime juice. Stir gently to combine.
2. Season: Add honey if using, and season with salt and pepper to taste. Thoroughly mix to ensure all the ingredients are dispersed evenly.
3. Chill: Place the relish in the refrigerator for at least half an hour before serving to let the flavors combine.
4. Serve: This relish is excellent served over grilled meats, with tacos, or as a refreshing addition to a salad.

Nutritional Information:
Calories: 70, Protein: 1 g, Carbohydrates: 15 g, Fat: 1 g, Fiber: 3 g, Cholesterol: 0 mg, Sodium: 5 mg, Potassium: 150 mg

Classic Apple Cider Vinegar Dressing

Ingredients

- 1/3 cup apple cider vinegar
- 2 tablespoons extra virgin olive oil
- 1 tablespoon Dijon mustard
- 1 tablespoon honey (optional, or adjust to taste)
- 1 clove garlic, minced
- Salt and freshly ground black pepper to taste

Directions

1. Whisk Ingredients: Combine the apple cider vinegar, olive oil, Dijon mustard, honey, and minced garlic in a small bowl and whisk until thoroughly blended and emulsified.
2. Season: Add salt and pepper to taste, adjusting the seasoning as needed.
3. Serve: Use immediately over your choice of salads, steamed vegetables, or as a marinade for poultry and fish.
4. Store: Pour the dressing into an airtight container and refrigerate for up to one week. Shake well before each use to recombine the ingredients.

Nutritional Information:
Calories: 100, Protein: 0 g, Carbohydrates: 3 g, Fat: 9 g, Fiber: 0 g, Cholesterol: 0 mg, Sodium: 50 mg, Potassium: 15 mg

Chimichurri Sauce

Ingredients

- 1 cup fresh flat-leaf parsley, tightly packed
- 3 cloves garlic, minced
- 2 tablespoons fresh oregano leaves (or 2 teaspoons dried oregano)
- 1/3 cup extra virgin olive oil
- 2 tablespoons red wine vinegar
- 1 tablespoon lime juice
- 1/2 teaspoon red pepper flakes
- Salt and pepper to taste

Directions

1. Chop Ingredients: Finely chop the parsley, garlic, and oregano. You can use a food processor, pulsing until finely chopped for a smoother texture.
2. Mix: In a bowl, combine the chopped herbs and garlic with olive oil, red wine vinegar, lime juice, and red pepper flakes.
3. Season: Season with salt and pepper to taste. If desired, adjust the acidity by adding more lime juice or vinegar.
4. Let Marinate: Before serving, let the sauce sit for at least 10 minutes to allow the flavors to combine.
5. Serve or Store: Use right away or store in an airtight container in the fridge for up to two weeks. The sauce is excellent on grilled meats, vegetables, or as a marinade.

Nutritional Information:
Calories: 170, Protein: 0.5 g, Carbohydrates: 3 g, Fat: 18 g, Fiber: 1 g, Cholesterol: 0 mg, Sodium: 80 mg, Potassium: 125 mg

Creamy Avocado Aioli

Prep. time:10 min | Cook time: 0 min | Serves: 4

Ingredients

- 1 ripe avocado
- 1 clove garlic, minced
- Juice of 1 lemon
- 2 tablespoons olive oil
- Salt and pepper to taste

Directions

1. Blend Ingredients: In a food processor or blender, combine the ripe avocado, minced garlic lemon juice, and olive oil. Blend until smooth and creamy.
2. Season: add salt and pepper to taste. Adjust the lemon juice or garlic according to your flavor preferences.
3. Chill: To allow the flavors to combine, place the aioli in the refrigerator for at least half an hour.
4. Serve: Use as a topping for grilled meats, a spread for sandwiches, or a dip for veggies.
5. Store: Store any leftovers in the refrigerator in an airtight container for up to two days.

Nutritional Information:
Calories: 140, Protein: 1 g, Carbohydrates: 5 g, Fat: 14 g, Fiber: 3 g, Cholesterol: 0 mg, Sodium: 5 mg, Potassium: 200 mg

Spicy Peanut Sauce

Prep. time: 5 min | Cook time: 0 min | Serves: 4

Ingredients

- 1/2 cup natural peanut butter (smooth or chunky based on preference)
- 2 tablespoons soy sauce (low sodium)
- 1 tablespoon lime juice
- 1 tablespoon of maple syrup or honey, sweetened to taste
- 1 clove garlic, minced
- 1 teaspoon grated fresh ginger
- 1/2 teaspoon red pepper flakes (adjust for heat preference)
- 1/4 cup warm water (to thin to desired consistency)

Directions

1. Ingredients: Combine peanut butter, soy sauce, lime juice, honey, maple syrup, ginger, garlic, and red pepper flakes in a mixing bowl.
2. Adjust Consistency: Add warm water while stirring until the sauce reaches your preferred consistency.
3. Taste and Adjust: Taste the sauce and adjust the seasoning g or sweetness as necessary. For more heat, add additional red pepper flakes.
4. Serve immediately with dishes like spring rolls, grilled meats, or as a vegetable dipping sauce.
5. Store: Refrigerate any leftover sauce in an airtight container for up to one week. Stir well before reuse, as separation may occur.

Nutritional Information:
Calories: 180, Protein: 7 g, Carbohydrates: 10 g, Fat: 14 g, Fiber: 2 g, Cholesterol: 0 mg, Sodium: 200 mg, Potassium: 200 mg

Chapter 11. Drinks and Smoothies

Green Goddess Detox Smoothie

Prep. time:10 min | Cook time: 0 min | Serves: 2

Ingredients

- 1 ripe banana
- 1/2 avocado, peeled and pitted
- 1 cup fresh spinach leaves
- 1/2 cucumber, chopped
- 1 celery stalk, chopped
- Juice of 1 lemon
- 1 tablespoon fresh ginger, grated
- 1 cup coconut water

Directions

1. Prepare Ingredients: Gather all your ingredients and prepare them as noted.
2. Blend Smoothly: In a blender, combine the banana, avocado, spinach, cucumber, celery, lemon juice, ginger, and coconut water. Blend on high until completely smooth.
3. Adjust Consistency: If the smoothie is too thick for your liking, add more coconut water and blend again to reach the desired consistency.
4. Taste and Adjust: Taste your smoothie and adjust the lemon or ginger for more zing.
5. Serve Immediately: Pour the smoothie into glasses and serve immediately for maximum freshness and nutrient intake.

Nutritional Information:
Calories: 160, Protein: 3 g, Carbohydrates: 30 g, Fat: 5 g, Fiber: 7 g, Cholesterol: 0 mg, Sodium: 60 mg, Potassium: 800 mg

Blueberry Oat Heart-Healthy Smoothie

Prep. time: 5 min | Cook time: 0 min | Serves: 2

Ingredients

- 1 cup fresh or frozen blueberries
- 1/2 cup rolled oats
- 1 banana
- 1 tablespoon chia seeds
- 1 cup almond milk (unsweetened)
- 1/2 cup Greek yogurt (plain, non-fat)
- 1 teaspoon honey (optional for sweetness)

Directions

1. Combine Ingredients: In a blender, combine blueberries, rolled oats, banana, chia seeds, almond milk, and Greek yogurt.
2. Blend: Blend on high speed until smooth. Remove the excess mixture by adding almond milk to get the right consistency.
3. Sweeten: Taste the smoothie and add honey if needed for additional sweetness.
4. Serve: Pour the smoothie into glasses and serve immediately for the freshest flavor and best nutrient retention.
5. Optional Garnish: Sprinkle a few extra oats or chia seeds on top for added texture and visual appeal.

Nutritional Information:
Calories: 210, Protein: 8 g, Carbohydrates: 38 g, Fat: 4 g, Fiber: 6 g, Cholesterol: 0 mg, Sodium: 55 mg, Potassium: 300 mg

Turmeric Ginger Tea

Prep. time: 5 min | Cook time: 10 min | Serves: 4

Ingredients

- 4 cups water
- 1 tablespoon fresh turmeric, grated (or 1 teaspoon ground turmeric)
- 1 tablespoon fresh ginger, grated
- Honey to taste (optional)
- Juice of half a lemon
- A pinch of black pepper (to enhance turmeric absorption)

Directions

1. Simmer: In a small saucepan, bring water to a boil. Add grated turmeric and ginger. Reduce heat and simmer for 10 minutes.
2. Strain: Strain the mixture into a large pitcher or directly into serving cups, removing the solid pieces of turmeric and ginger.
3. Flavor Enhancements: Stir in honey (if used) and lemon juice to taste. Add a pinch of black pepper to each cup.
4. Serve: Serve the tea warm or let it cool down and enjoy it as a refreshing, cold beverage.
5. Store: If there are leftovers, store them in the refrigerator and enjoy them within 24 hours for the best flavor and health benefits.

Nutritional Information:
Calories: 9, Protein: 0 g, Carbohydrates: 2 g, Fat: 0 g, Fiber: 0 g, Cholesterol: 0 mg, Sodium: 12 mg, Potassium: 50 mg

Pomegranate Antioxidant Blast

Prep. time: 10 min | Cook time: 0 min | Serves: 4

Ingredients

- 2 cups pomegranate seeds
- 1 cup fresh orange juice
- 1 banana, sliced
- 1/2 cup frozen mixed berries (such as blueberries, raspberries, and blackberries)
- One tablespoon of chia seeds
- Ice cubes (optional for serving chilled)

Directions

1. Blend Ingredients: In a blender, combine the pomegranate seeds, orange juice, banana, mixed berries, and chia seeds. Blend until smooth.
2. Strain (Optional): To achieve a smoother texture, strain the mixture to remove the pulp using a fine-mesh sieve or cheesecloth.
3. Adjust Consistency: If the smoothie is too thick, add more orange juice or water to reach the desired consistency.
4. Serve: Pour into glasses over ice if desired for a refreshing, chilled drink.
5. Garnish: Sprinkle a few pomegranate seeds or a dash of chia seeds on top before serving for an extra touch of nutrition and visual appeal.

Nutritional Information:
Calories: 150, Protein: 2 g, Carbohydrates: 35 g, Fat: 2 g, Fiber: 4 g, Cholesterol: 0 mg, Sodium: 5 mg, Potassium: 400 mg

Almond Milk Chai Latte

Prep. time: 5 min | Cook time: 10 min | Serves: 4

Ingredients

- 4 cups unsweetened almond milk
- 2 cinnamon sticks
- 6 cardamom pods, slightly crushed
- 4 cloves
- 2 slices fresh ginger
- 2 black tea bags
- 2 tablespoons honey or to taste

Directions

1. Simmer Spices: In a medium saucepan, combine almond milk, cinnamon sticks, cardamom pods, cloves, and ginger slices. Bring the mixture to a gentle simmer over low heat, being careful not to boil.
2. Steep Tea: Once simmering, add the tea bags, remove the saucepan from heat, and let steep for about 5 minutes.
3. Sweeten: Strain the tea bags and spices. Stir in honey to sweeten the latte to your liking.
4. Serve: Divide the chai latte among mugs. Serve hot, and for an extra touch, sprinkle a little ground cinnamon on top before serving.
5. Store: Any leftovers can be stored in the refrigerator and reheated gently on the stove or enjoyed cold.

Nutritional Information:
Calories: 60, Protein: 1 g, Carbohydrates: 10 g, Fat: 2.5 g, Fiber: 1 g, Cholesterol: 0 mg, Sodium: 180 mg, Potassium: 50 mg

Cucumber Mint Refresh

Prep. time: 10 min | Cook time: 0 min | Serves: 4

Ingredients

- 1 large cucumber, peeled and chopped
- Juice of 2 limes
- 1/4 cup fresh mint leaves
- 2 tablespoons honey (optional, adjust to taste)
- 4 cups cold water or sparkling water for a fizzy twist
- Ice cubes for serving

Directions

1. Blend Ingredients: In a blender, combine the chopped cucumber, lime juice, mint leaves, and honey. Blend until smooth.
2. Strain Mixture: Strain the mixture through a fine mesh sieve into a pitcher to remove the solids and ensure a smooth drink.
3. Add Water: Stir in cold or sparkling water to the cucumber mixture. Mix well to combine.
4. Chill and Serve: Fill glasses with ice and pour the cucumber mint refreshment over them. Garnish with additional mint leaves or cucumber slices, if desired.
5. Adjust Flavors: Taste and adjust the sweetness with more honey if needed, or add more lime juice for extra zing.

Nutritional Information:
Calories: 25, Protein: 0.5 g, Carbohydrates: 6 g, Fat: 0 g, Fiber: 0.5 g, Cholesterol: 0 mg, Sodium: 10 mg, Potassium: 75 mg

Cherry Almond Protein Smoothie

Prep. time: 5min | Cook time: 0 min | Serves: 4

Ingredients

- 2 cups frozen cherries
- 1 banana, sliced
- 1/4 cup almond butter
- 2 cups almond milk (unsweetened)
- 1 scoop vanilla or plain protein powder (your choice of whey or plant-based)
- 1 tablespoon flaxseed meal
- Ice cubes (optional, depending on preferred consistency)

Directions

1. Combine Ingredients: Add the frozen cherries, banana, almond butter, almond milk, protein powder, and flaxseed meal to a blender.
2. Blend: Blend on high until smooth. Add ice cubes if you prefer a colder or thicker smoothie, and blend again.
3. Taste and Adjust: If the smoothie doesn't taste sweet enough, combine it again after adding a little honey or maple syrup.
4. Serve: For optimal flavor and nutrient retention, pour the smoothie into glasses and serve immediately.
5. Garnish Optional: Garnish with a few cherry pieces or a sprinkle of ground almonds for an extra touch.

Nutritional Information:
Calories: 280, Protein: 10 g, Carbohydrates: 30 g, Fat: 15 g, Fiber: 5 g, Cholesterol: 0 mg, Sodium: 180 mg, Potassium: 500 mg

Lemon Ginger Flush Drink

Prep. time: 10 min | Cook time: 0 min | Serves: 4

Ingredients

- 4 cups water
- Juice of 2 lemons
- 2 inches of freshly peeled and finely sliced ginger root
- 1 tablespoon honey (optional for sweetness)
- A pinch of cayenne pepper (optional for a metabolic boost)

Directions

1. Prepare Ingredients: In a large pitcher, combine the water, freshly squeezed lemon juice, and sliced ginger.
2. Chill: For more pronounced flavors, allow the mixture to infuse in the refrigerator for at least an hour or overnight.
3. Sweeten and Spice: Before serving, stir in honey to taste, if desired, and a pinch of cayenne pepper for a bit of heat.
4. Serve: Pour the drink over ice in glasses. If preferred, strain to remove ginger slices.
5. Garnish: Garnish with a lemon slice or a small sprig of mint for an extra touch of freshness.

Nutritional Information:
Calories: 25, Protein: 0 g, Carbohydrates: 7 g, Fat: 0 g, Fiber: 0 g, Cholesterol: 0 mg, Sodium: 5 mg, Potassium: 49 mg

Carrot and Orange Immune Booster

Prep. time: 10 min | Cook time: 0 min | Serves: 4

Ingredients

- 4 large carrots, peeled and chopped
- 4 oranges, peeled and sectioned
- 1-inch piece of fresh ginger, peeled
- 1 teaspoon turmeric powder (optional for added anti-inflammatory benefits)
- Ice cubes (optional for serving)

Directions

1. Juice the Ingredients: Use a juicer to process the carrots, orange sections, and ginger pieces. Ensure everything is well juiced.
2. Enhance with turmeric: Stir the turmeric powder into the j ice and mix well to combine. Turmeric is optional but recommended for its health benefits.
3. Chill: Pour the juice into a pitcher and refrigerate until chilled, or serve immediately over ice in glasses.
4. Stir Before Serving: Give the juice a good stir before serving to ensure all the flavors are well combined.
5. Garnish: Garnish with a small sprig of mint or an orange slice for a decorative touch.

Nutritional Information:
Calories: 120, Protein: 2 g, Carbohydrates: 29 g, Fat: 0.5 g, Fiber: 6 g, Cholesterol: 0 mg, Sodium: 60 mg, Potassium: 490 mg

Spinach and Kiwi Smoothie

Prep. time: 5 min | Cook time: 0 min | Serves: 4

Ingredients

- 2 ripe kiwis, peeled and sliced
- 2 cups fresh spinach leaves
- 1 banana, sliced
- 1/2 cup Greek yogurt or non-dairy yogurt for a vegan option
- 1 cup unsweetened almond milk
- 1 tablespoon honey or agave syrup (optional for sweetness)
- Ice cubes (optional for a colder smoothie)

Directions

1. Combine Ingredients: Add the kiwi slices, spinach, banana, yogurt, and almond milk to a blender.
2. Blend Smoothly: Blend on high until all components are thoroughly combined, and the mixture is smooth.
3. Adjust Consistency: To get the right consistency, add almond milk to thin out any extra smoothie. If you prefer it colder, blend it with ice cubes.
4. Sweeten if Desired: Taste the smoothie; if you prefer it sweeter, add honey or agave syrup and blend again to mix well.
5. Serve Immediately: Pour the smoothie into glasses and serve immediately to enjoy its freshness and nutritional benefits.

Nutritional Information:
Calories: 110, Protein: 4 g, Carbohydrates: 20 g, Fat: 1.5 g, Fiber: 3 g, Cholesterol: 0 mg, Sodium: 55 mg, Potassium: 420 mg

Matcha Green Tea Latte

Prep. time: 5 min | Cook time: 0 min | Serves: 2

Ingredients

- 1 teaspoon matcha green tea powder
- 1 tablespoon hot water (not boiling)
- 2 cups unsweetened almond milk or any other milk of choice
- 1-2 teaspoons honey or another sweetener of choice (optional)
- Ice cubes (for the iced version)

Directions

1. Dissolve Matcha: Mix the matcha green tea powder with the boiling water in a small bowl until a homogeneous paste forms.
2. Heat the Milk: In a small saucepan, gently heat the almond milk until hot but not boiling, or use a microwave for about 45 seconds.
3. Combine: Add the matcha paste to the milk. If using sweetener, add it as well. Whisk vigorously until the mixture is bubbly.
4. Serve: For a hot latte, pour the mixture into cups and enjoy immediately. Let the mixture cool slightly for an iced version, then pour over ice in glasses.
5. Garnish: Optionally, sprinkle a little matcha powder on top for garnish.

Nutritional Information:
Calories: 70, Protein: 2 g, Carbohydrates: 6 g, Fat: 4 g, Fiber: 1 g, Cholesterol: 0 mg, Sodium: 180 mg, Potassium: 50 mg

Pineapple Coconut Water Smoothie

Prep. time: 5 min | Cook time: 0 min | Serves: 4

Ingredients

- 2 cups fresh pineapple chunks
- 1 cup coconut water
- 1 banana
- 1/2 cup Greek yogurt (use non-dairy yogurt for vegan option)
- 1/2 cup ice cubes
- 1 tablespoon honey or agave syrup (optional)
-

Directions

1. Blend Ingredients: Combine pineapple chunks, coconut water, banana, yogurt, and ice cubes in a blender.
2. Smooth Consistency: Blend on high until smooth.
3. Adjust Sweetness: Taste and add honey or agave syrup if a sweeter taste is desired, then blend again.
4. Serve Immediately: Pour the smoothie into glasses and serve immediately to enjoy its maximum freshness and flavor.
5. Optional Garnish: Garnish with a slice of pineapple or a sprig of mint for a decorative touch.

Nutritional Information:
Calories: 120, Protein: 2 g, Carbohydrates: 28 g, Fat: 0.5 g, Fiber: 2 g, Cholesterol: 0 mg, Sodium: 30 mg, Potassium: 300 mg

Peppermint and Lemon Digestive Aid Tea

Prep. time: 5 min | Cook time: 10 min | Serves: 4

Ingredients

- 4 cups water
- 2 tablespoons dried peppermint leaves or 4 peppermint tea bags
- 1 lemon, juiced and zested
- 1 tablespoon honey (optional)

Directions

1. Boil Water: Heat the water in a medium saucepan until it boils.
2. Steep Tea: Add the dried peppermint leaves or tea bags and the zest to the boiling water. Remove from heat and let it steep for 10 minutes.
3. Add Lemon and Honey: Strain the mixture to remove leaves or tea bags. Stir in fresh lemon juice and honey, if using, until well mixed.
4. Serve: Once the tea is hot, pour it into glasses.
5. Garnish Option: For an extra touch of flavor, garnish with a slice of lemon or a fresh peppermint leaf.

Nutritional Information:
Calories: 10, Protein: 0 g, Carbohydrates: 3 g, Fat: 0 g, Fiber: 0 g, Cholesterol: 0 mg, Sodium: 2 mg, Potassium: 20 mg

Avocado and Lime Smoothie

Prep. time: 5 min | Cook time: 0 min | Serves: 4

Ingredients

- 1 ripe avocado, peeled and pitted
- 2 limes, juiced
- 1 cup unsweetened almond milk
- 1/2 cup Greek yogurt or non-dairy yogurt
- 2 tablespoons honey or agave syrup (optional)
- 1 cup ice cubes

Directions

1. Blend Ingredients: Combine the avocado, lime juice, almond milk, yogurt, and ice cubes in a blender.
2. Adjust Sweetness: If you desire a sweeter taste, add honey or agave syrup and blend until smooth.
3. Check Consistency: If the smoothie is too thick, add a bit extra almond milk to get the right consistency.
4. Serve Right Away: Pour the smoothie into glasses and serve immediately to ensure the most incredible texture and freshness.
5. Optional garnish: For an extra zesty touch, garnish with a lime slice or a sprig of mint.

Nutritional Information:
Calories: 160, Protein: 4 g, Carbohydrates: 18 g, Fat: 10 g, Fiber: 5 g, Cholesterol: 0 mg, Sodium: 40 mg, Potassium: 450 mg

Chapter 12. 60-Day Meal Plan

	BREAKFAST	SNACK	LUNCH	DINNER
Day 1	Avocado Toast with Tomatoes	Roasted Chickpea Poppers	Greek Salad with Olives	Herb-Roasted Chicken Breast with Garlic Roasted Green Beans
Day 2	Oatmeal with Berries and Almonds	Fig and Ricotta Crostinis	Lentil and Spinach Soup	Lemon Garlic Shrimp over Whole-Wheat Pasta
Day 3	Banana Pancakes	Sweet Potato and Beet Chips	Mediterranean Chickpea Salad with Herbs	Spiced Orange Chicken Skewers with Spiced Pumpkin Puree
Day 4	Quinoa and Berry Breakfast Bowl	Avocado and Tomato Bruschetta	Pumpkin and Coconut Soup	Balsamic Glazed Beef Skewers with Lemon-Garlic Asparagus Spears
Day 5	Banana Nut Smoothie	Tomato and Basil Skewers	Avocado and Grapefruit Salad with Citrus Vinaigrette	Honey Garlic Baked Trout with Citrusy Roasted Broccoli
Day 6	Chia Pudding Parfait	Zucchini and Corn Fritters	Tomato Basil and Mozzarella Salad	Chickpea and Spinach Curry with Minted Zucchini and Pea Salad
Day 7	Smoothie with Chia Seeds and Kiwi	Edamame and Garlic Dip	Carrot and Ginger Puree Soup	Garlic Lime Chicken Tenders with Roasted Brussels Sprouts with Pomegranate
Day 8	Mediterranean Veggie Omelette	Crispy Kale Chips	Beetroot and Goat Cheese Arugula Salad	Grilled Salmon with Lemon Pepper and Cumin-Spiced Carrot Fries
Day 9	Greek Yogurt with Honey and Nuts	Chia Seed and Berry Yogurt Parfaits	Vegetable Soup	Beef Tenderloin with Roasted Tomatoes and Creamy Cauliflower Mash
Day 10	Egg White Veggie Scramble	Sweet Potato and Beet Chips	Mediterranean Couscous Salad	Vegan Mushroom Stroganoff with Grilled Eggplant with Fresh Herbs
Day 11	Avocado Toast with Tomatoes	Tomato and Basil Skewers	Lentil and Spinach Soup	Spicy Tomato Beef Tacos with Tangy Tomato and Cucumber Salad
Day 12	Oatmeal with Berries and Almonds	Stuffed Cherry Tomatoes	Greek Salad with Olives	Lemon Garlic Shrimp over Whole-Wheat Pasta

	BREAKFAST	SNACK	LUNCH	DINNER
Day 13	Banana Pancakes	Fig and Ricotta Crostinis	Mediterranean Chickpea Salad with Herbs	Pesto Grilled Shrimp with Summer Squash and Roasted Brussels Sprouts with Pomegranate
Day 14	Quinoa and Berry Breakfast Bowl	Avocado and Tomato Bruschetta	Pumpkin and Coconut Soup	Balsamic Glazed Chicken Drumsticks with Roasted Brussels Sprouts
Day 15	Banana Nut Smoothie	Crispy Kale Chips	Tomato Basil and Mozzarella Salad	Spiced Orange Chicken Skewers with Lemon-Garlic Asparagus Spears
Day 16	Chia Pudding Parfait	Zucchini and Corn Fritters	Carrot and Ginger Puree Soup	Balsamic Glazed Beef Skewers with Creamy Cauliflower Mash
Day 17	Smoothie with Chia Seeds and Kiwi	Sweet Potato and Beet Chips	Avocado and Grapefruit Salad with Citrus Vinaigrette	Honey Garlic Baked Trout with Roasted Brussels Sprouts with Pomegranate
Day 18	Mediterranean Veggie Omelette	Tomato and Basil Skewers	Beetroot and Goat Cheese Arugula Salad	Grilled Salmon with Lemon Pepper and Cumin-Spiced Carrot Fries
Day 19	Greek Yogurt with Honey and Nuts	Edamame and Garlic Dip	Lentil and Spinach Soup	Spicy Tomato Beef Tacos with Citrusy Roasted Broccoli
Day 20	Egg White Veggie Scramble	Crispy Kale Chips	Greek Salad with Olives	Pesto Grilled Shrimp with Summer Squash and Roasted Brussels Sprouts with Pomegranate
Day 21	Avocado Toast with Tomatoes	Sweet Potato and Beet Chips	Mediterranean Chickpea Salad with Herbs	Balsamic Glazed Chicken Drumsticks with Lemon-Garlic Asparagus Spears
Day 22	Oatmeal with Berries and Almonds	Fig and Ricotta Crostinis	Pumpkin and Coconut Soup	Beef Tenderloin with Roasted Tomatoes and Creamy Cauliflower Mash
Day 23	Oatmeal with Berries and Almonds	Fig and Ricotta Crostinis	Pumpkin and Coconut Soup	Beef Tenderloin with Roasted Tomatoes and Creamy Cauliflower Mash
Day 24	Banana Pancakes	Stuffed Cherry Tomatoes	Tomato Basil and Mozzarella Salad	Lemon Garlic Shrimp over Whole-Wheat Pasta
Day 25	Quinoa and Berry Breakfast Bowl	Zucchini and Corn Fritters	Carrot and Ginger Puree Soup	Vegan Mushroom Stroganoff with Grilled Eggplant with Fresh Herbs

	BREAKFAST	SNACK	LUNCH	DINNER
Day 26	Banana Nut Smoothie	Avocado and Tomato Bruschetta	Avocado and Grapefruit Salad with Citrus Vinaigrette	Garlic Lime Chicken Tenders with Roasted Brussels Sprouts with Pomegranate
Day 27	Chia Pudding Parfait	Tomato and Basil Skewers	Lentil and Spinach Soup	Spicy Tomato Beef Tacos with Tangy Tomato and Cucumber Salad
Day 28	Smoothie with Chia Seeds and Kiwi	Sweet Potato and Beet Chips	Greek Salad with Olives	Balsamic Glazed Beef Skewers with Creamy Cauliflower Mash
Day 29	Mediterranean Veggie Omelette	Crispy Kale Chips	Beetroot and Goat Cheese Arugula Salad	Grilled Salmon with Lemon Pepper and Cumin-Spiced Carrot Fries
Day 30	Greek Yogurt with Honey and Nuts	Edamame and Garlic Dip	Carrot and Ginger Puree Soup	Spicy Tomato Beef Tacos with Citrusy Roasted Broccoli
Day 31	Egg White Veggie Scramble	Fig and Ricotta Crostinis	Mediterranean Chickpea Salad with Herbs	Pesto Grilled Shrimp with Summer Squash and Roasted Brussels Sprouts with Pomegranate
Day 32	Avocado Toast with Tomatoes	Sweet Potato and Beet Chips	Pumpkin and Coconut Soup	Beef Tenderloin with Roasted Tomatoes and Creamy Cauliflower Mash
Day 33	Oatmeal with Berries and Almonds	Zucchini and Corn Fritters	Greek Salad with Olives	Lemon Garlic Shrimp over Whole-Wheat Pasta
Day 34	Banana Pancakes	Tomato and Basil Skewers	Avocado and Grapefruit Salad with Citrus Vinaigrette	Garlic Lime Chicken Tenders with Roasted Brussels Sprouts with Pomegranate
Day 35	Quinoa and Berry Breakfast Bowl	Stuffed Cherry Tomatoes	Carrot and Ginger Puree Soup	Vegan Mushroom Stroganoff with Grilled Eggplant with Fresh Herbs
Day 36	Banana Nut Smoothie	Sweet Potato and Beet Chips	Lentil and Spinach Soup	Balsamic Glazed Chicken Drumsticks with Lemon-Garlic Asparagus Spears
Day 37	Chia Pudding Parfait	Edamame and Garlic Dip	Tomato Basil and Mozzarella Salad	Pesto Grilled Shrimp with Summer Squash and Roasted Brussels Sprouts with Pomegranate
Day 38	Mediterranean Veggie Omelette	Fig and Ricotta Crostinis	Carrot and Ginger Puree Soup	Beef Tenderloin with Roasted Tomatoes and Creamy Cauliflower Mash

	BREAKFAST	SNACK	LUNCH	DINNER
Day 39	Greek Yogurt with Honey and Nuts	Tomato and Basil Skewers	Greek Salad with Olives	Lemon Garlic Shrimp over Whole-Wheat Pasta
Day 40	Egg White Veggie Scramble	Sweet Potato and Beet Chips	Avocado and Grapefruit Salad with Citrus Vinaigrette	Garlic Lime Chicken Tenders with Roasted Brussels Sprouts with Pomegranate
Day 41	Avocado Toast with Tomatoes	Zucchini and Corn Fritters	Pumpkin and Coconut Soup	Vegan Mushroom Stroganoff with Grilled Eggplant with Fresh Herbs
Day 42	Oatmeal with Berries and Almonds	Crispy Kale Chips	Lentil and Spinach Soup	Balsamic Glazed Chicken Drumsticks with Lemon-Garlic Asparagus Spears
Day 43	Banana Pancakes	Edamame and Garlic Dip	Greek Salad with Olives	Beef Tenderloin with Roasted Tomatoes and Creamy Cauliflower Mash
Day 44	Quinoa and Berry Breakfast Bowl	Fig and Ricotta Crostinis	Avocado and Grapefruit Salad with Citrus Vinaigrette	Pesto Grilled Shrimp with Summer Squash and Roasted Brussels Sprouts with Pomegranate
Day 45	Banana Nut Smoothie	Sweet Potato and Beet Chips	Carrot and Ginger Puree Soup	Lemon Garlic Shrimp over Whole-Wheat Pasta
Day 46	Chia Pudding Parfait	Tomato and Basil Skewers	Lentil and Spinach Soup	Garlic Lime Chicken Tenders with Roasted Brussels Sprouts with Pomegranate
Day 47	Smoothie with Chia Seeds and Kiwi	Crispy Kale Chips	Greek Salad with Olives	Spicy Tomato Beef Tacos with Citrusy Roasted Broccoli
Day 48	Mediterranean Veggie Omelette	Zucchini and Corn Fritters	Pumpkin and Coconut Soup	Beef Tenderloin with Roasted Tomatoes and Creamy Cauliflower Mash
Day 49	Greek Yogurt with Honey and Nuts	Fig and Ricotta Crostinis	Tomato Basil and Mozzarella Salad	Pesto Grilled Shrimp with Summer Squash and Roasted Brussels Sprouts with Pomegranate
Day 50	Egg White Veggie Scramble	Sweet Potato and Beet Chips	Avocado and Grapefruit Salad with Citrus Vinaigrette	Lemon Garlic Shrimp over Whole-Wheat Pasta

	BREAKFAST	SNACK	LUNCH	DINNER
Day 51	Avocado Toast with Tomatoes	Tomato and Basil Skewers	Lentil and Spinach Soup	Garlic Lime Chicken Tenders with Roasted Brussels Sprouts with Pomegranate
Day 52	Oatmeal with Berries and Almonds	Crispy Kale Chips	Greek Salad with Olives	Vegan Mushroom Stroganoff with Grilled Eggplant with Fresh Herbs
Day 53	Banana Pancakes	Fig and Ricotta Crostinis	Avocado and Grapefruit Salad with Citrus Vinaigrette	Beef Tenderloin with Roasted Tomatoes and Creamy Cauliflower Mash
Day 54	Quinoa and Berry Breakfast Bowl	Edamame and Garlic Dip	Carrot and Ginger Puree Soup	Lemon Garlic Shrimp over Whole-Wheat Pasta
Day 55	Banana Nut Smoothie	Tomato and Basil Skewers	Lentil and Spinach Soup	Garlic Lime Chicken Tenders with Roasted Brussels Sprouts with Pomegranate
Day 56	Chia Pudding Parfait	Sweet Potato and Beet Chips	Greek Salad with Olives	Pesto Grilled Shrimp with Summer Squash and Roasted Brussels Sprouts with Pomegranate
Day 57	Smoothie with Chia Seeds and Kiwi	Fig and Ricotta Crostinis	Pumpkin and Coconut Soup	Beef Tenderloin with Roasted Tomatoes and Creamy Cauliflower Mash
Day 58	Mediterranean Veggie Omelette	Tomato and Basil Skewers	Carrot and Ginger Puree Soup	Spicy Tomato Beef Tacos with Citrusy Roasted Broccoli
Day 59	Greek Yogurt with Honey and Nuts	Sweet Potato and Beet Chips	Greek Salad with Olives	Lemon Garlic Shrimp over Whole-Wheat Pasta
Day 60	Egg White Veggie Scramble	Crispy Kale Chips	Avocado and Grapefruit Salad with Citrus Vinaigrette	Garlic Lime Chicken Tenders with Roasted Brussels Sprouts with Pomegranate

This plan ensures variety and balance, covering different types of meals, including vegetarian, vegan, and meat options. Feel free to adjust the plan based on personal preferences and nutritional needs.

Chapter 13. Shopping list

Embracing a low-cholesterol diet begins at the supermarket. By filling your cart with the right ingredients, you can cook meals that can quickly lower cholesterol and strengthen heart health. This chapter provides a comprehensive shopping list to guide you through choosing the best foods that align with a heart-healthy lifestyle.

Fruits and Vegetables

Fruits and vegetables are foundational to a low-cholesterol diet. They are rich in fiber, vitamins, and antioxidants but naturally low in fat and cholesterol.

- Apples
- Berries (blueberries, strawberries, raspberries)
- Citrus fruits (oranges, lemons, grapefruits)
- Pears
- Bananas
- Leafy greens (spinach, kale, Swiss chard)
- Broccoli
- Carrots
- Bell peppers
- Tomatoes
- Avocados
- Sweet potatoes

- Eggplants
- Garlic and onions

Whole Grains

Whole grains are excellent sources of fiber, which can help reduce cholesterol absorption in your bloodstream.

- Oats (old-fashioned or steel-cut)
- Barley
- Whole wheat bread and pasta
- Brown rice
- Quinoa
- Bulgur

Proteins

Choosing lean proteins and plant-based options can significantly affect cholesterol levels and heart health.

- Legumes (beans, lentils, chickpeas)
- Fish (salmon, mackerel, trout, sardines)
- Skinless poultry (chicken or turkey breast)
- Lean cuts of meat (choose "loin" and "round" cuts and trim visible fat)
- Egg whites or cholesterol-free egg substitutes
- Nuts and seeds (almonds, walnuts, flaxseeds, chia seeds)

Dairy or Dairy Alternatives

Low-fat or non-fat dairy products provide essential nutrients without the added cholesterol.

- Skim or 1% milk
- Low-fat or non-fat yogurt
- Low-fat cheese
- Plant-based milk (almond, soy, oat)

Fats and Oils

Healthy fats are crucial for overall health and can help manage cholesterol levels.

- Olive oil
- Canola oil
- Avocado oil
- Flaxseed oil
- Nuts and natural nut butter

Condiments and Spices

Spices and other flavorings are a healthy way to add excitement to your dishes without extra cholesterol.

- Herbs (fresh or dried like basil, parsley, thyme)
- Spices (turmeric, cinnamon, ginger)
- Vinegar (apple cider, balsamic)
- Low-sodium soy sauce
- Mustard
- Nutritional yeast

Tips for Shopping

1. Stick to the outer aisles of the grocery store, where fresh foods such as fruits, vegetables, and refrigerated items are typically located.
2. Read labels carefully to manage your intake of saturated fats, trans fats, and sodium.
3. Plan your meals ahead to ensure you buy only what you need, reduce waste, and adhere to your diet.
4. Buy whole grains and legumes in bulk to save money and time in the long run.

By following this shopping list and advice, you'll be well on your way to cooking delicious, heart-healthy meals to help keep your cholesterol in check.

Measurement conversations

Dry Measurements Conversion Chart

Teaspoons	Tablespoons	Cups
3 tsp	1 tbsp	1/16 c
6 tsp	2 tbsp	1/8 c
12 tsp	4 tbsp	1/4 c
24 tsp	8 tbsp	1/2 c
36 tsp	12 tbsp	3/4 c
48 tsp	16 tbsp	1 c

Liquid Measurements Conversion Chart

Fluid Ounces	Cups	Pints	Quarts	Gallons
8 fl. oz	1 c	1/2 pt	1/4 qt	1/16 gal
16 fl. oz	2 c	1 pt	1/2 qt	1/8 gal
32 fl. oz	4 c	2 pt	1 qt	1/4 gal
64 fl. oz	8 c	4 pt	2 qt	1/2 gal
128 fl. oz	16 c	8 pt	4 qt	1 gal

Liquid Measurements (Volume)

Metric	Standard
1 mL	1/5 tsp
5 mL	1 tsp
15 mL	1 tbsp
240 mL	1 c (8 fl. oz)
1 liter	34 fl. oz

Dry Measurements (Weight)

Metric	Standard
1 g	.035 oz
100 g	3.5 oz
500 g	17.7 oz (1.1 lb)
1 kg	35 oz

US to Metric Conversions

Standard	Metric
1/5 tsp	1 ml
1 tsp	5 ml
1 tbsp	15 ml
1 fl. oz	30 ml
1 c	237 ml
1 pt	473 ml
1 qt	.95 l
1 gal	3.8 l
1 oz	28 g
1 lb	454 g

Oven Temperature Conversion

Celsius	Fahrenheit
120 C	250 F
160 C	320 F
180 C	350 F
205 C	400 F
220 C	425 F

1 CUP

1 cup = 8 fluid ounces
1 cup = 16 tablespoons
1 cup = 48 teaspoons
1 cup = ½ pint
1 cup = ¼ quart
1 cup = 1/16 gallon
1 cup = 240 ml

Recipe Index